INFORMATION TECHNOLOGY
A Revolutionary Change

INFORMATION TECHNOLOGY
A Revolutionary Change
(In 9 Volumes)

Volume 8
(On the Road to Electronic Environment)

Editor
RAMESH CHANDRA
Vice-Chancellor, Bundelkhand University, Jhansi (U.P.)

KALPAZ PUBLICATIONS
DELHI–110052

INFORMATION TECHNOLOGY: A REVOLUTIONARY CHANGE
(Information Technology)

Rs. 8000 (Set)
Rs. 900 (Each Volume)

ISBN: 81-7835-201-X (Set)
ISBN: 81-7835-227-3 (Vol. 8)

Published in 2003 in India by
Kalpaz Publications
C–30, Satyawati Nagar
Delhi–110052
E-mail: kalpaz@hotmail.com

Laser Typesetting at: Varsha Graphics, Delhi
Printed at: Mehra Offset Printers, New Delhi

Contents

Preface

Today, computers and other electronic devices increasingly communicate and interact directly with other devices over a variety of networks, such as the Internet. The information and communication technologies (ICT) are central to the creation of the emerging global knowledge-based economy and can play an important role in accelerating growth, in promoting sustainable development and eradicating poverty in developing countries as well as countries with economies in transition and in facilitating their effective integration into the global economy.

The new technologies can shape and enhance a wide range of development applications —from e-commerce to access to financial markets; from generating employment to providing opportunities for investment to entrepreneurs, in particular small and medium-sized enterprises; from improved agricultural and manufacturing productivity to the empowerment of all sections of society; from long-distance education to tele-medicine; from environmental management and monitoring to prevention and management of disasters. Access to information and knowledge-sharing is largely determined by education, capabilities, including resources, transparent societies, capacity to generate and utilize knowledge, connectivity and the availability of diverse content and applications, and the policy and legal/regulatory framework. Efforts to achieve universal connectivity, particularly at the lower income levels, in all countries and especially in developing countries, will require innovative approaches and partnerships, including group and community connectivity and private-sector investment. In this regard, the establishment of integrated multipurpose and multimedia community information centres will be important.

Effective and meaningful collaborative efforts are required, involving Governments, multilateral development institutions, bilateral donors, the private sector, civil society and other relevant stakeholders, to enhance the developmental impact of ICT. Such efforts should include transfer of technology to developing countries on concessional and preferential terms, as mutually agreed, especially technology related to knowledge-based sectors, the mobilization of resources from all sources, public and private, at the national and international levels, and promoting capacity-building.

Editor

1

Technology in Electronic Environment

Today, computers and other electronic devices increasingly communicate and interact directly with other devices over a variety of networks, such as the Internet. Consumers and businesses have been particularly quick to recognize the potential and realize the benefits of adopting new computer-enabled networks. Consumers now routinely use computer networks to identify sellers, evaluate products and services, compare prices, and exert market leverage.

Businesses use networks even more extensively to conduct and re-engineer production processes, streamline procurement processes, reach new customers, and manage internal operations. This electronic revolution in economy is spurring additional investments in facilities, hardware, software, services, and human capital. Ultimately, it may change the structure and performance of the American economy as much as the introduction of the computer a generation ago. While the burgeoning use of electronic devices in economy is widely acknowledged and discussed, it remains largely undefined and unrecognized in official economic statistics.

Telecommunication Revolution

Telecommunications is a growth industry and also will be moving towards a horizontal structure. The greatest opportunities for established carriers are likely to be in providing network outsourcing services. The changes required to exploit these opportunities will be major, and it is very likely that there will be huge bankruptcies and writedowns. However, the telecom industry, as measured by revenues, is likely to grow, as it has in the past. There will be greater diversity in available communication services, which should provide for a more resilient infrastructure, even when individual companies restructure.

The telecom crash that started in the year 2000 has been brutal to the traditional long distance carriers and devastating to the new carriers, whether in local or long distance segments of the market. The telecom crash was a crash only for the telecom suppliers, the result of an unsustainable explosion in capital expenditures. Total revenues of service providers have been growing all along at rates of 5 to 10% a year for the whole sector, with some companies going out of business, while others boom. That rate of growth is very respectable, and, following historical precedent, faster than the growth rate of the economy as a whole.

The crash occurred because even this fast growth rate was simply not sufficient to sustain the boom in capital expenditures. The growth of the entire telecom pie allows for relatively gentle transformations. In particular, new services can grow without destroying old ones. That has been the historical pattern, and can be seen today. There is much public concern about the slow spread of broadband in the US. Yet, with the number of households with DSL or cable modems about tripling in 2001, that rate is quite fast, certainly by comparison with the spread of cell phones.

Some countries have experienced much faster broadband penetration, but then their prices have been much lower. For a service that costs $40-50 a month, the US is not doing too badly in speed of broadband adoption. Lower price would certainly increase US penetration, but this price sensitivity just reinforces the point that the perceived utility of broadband is not all that great, at least not yet. At a low enough price, people will buy just to get a modestly improved performance with email. At the higher price that prevails in the US, consumers have to be convinced that the higher bandwidth and the always-on capability provide real value, and that takes time.

Of course, in a low marginal cost business such as telecommunications, even a drop of 8% is noticeable, and would surely be reflected in stock market valuation of the companies. The main issue is whether some compensating sources of revenues can be developed in the meantime. New technologies, such as wavelength switching, are on the horizon, and will surely transform the industry. However, that will take time.

The telecommunications industry is extremely complex. What is beyond dispute, though, is that most of the costs are at the edges of the network. Furthermore, technology over the last two decades has been shifting the balance of costs even further towards the edges than before. The main reason the established long distance carriers have been suffering is that their consumer voice business is not viable. When the Bell System was broken up, long distance transport was still expensive.

However, for several years now wholesale prices for long distance voice calls in the US have been under a penny a minute. Those costs and a competitive marketplace are not compatible in the long run with consumer prices that are 10 times as high. It was inevitable that for ordinary customers, long distance was eventually going to be provided by their local carriers on a flat rate basis. The decline in long distance transport costs that doomed consumer long distance voice carriers predated the Internet.

However, the Internet helped speed up the transformation we are witnessing by leading to the wild overbuilding of long distance transport and by accelerating technical advances. The costs on the Internet are even more heavily concentrated at the edges, especially if one considers the Internet as just a component of the entire IT infrastructure. The electronics have been getting less expensive, but the labor has not, and in particular the costs of the final few hundred feet of a connection to the network have been remarkably stable and remarkably high.

After all, most households do have three separate communication systems, the copper-based one from their ILEC, a coax-based one from their cable TV provider, and a cell phone from a wireless carrier. Thus a much deeper look is needed to understand what is going on. A key factor is that change is slow but inevitable. Hence a static analysis of technology choices, without taking account how quickly consumer are likely to move, is bound to be inadequate. In particular, whether DSL or cable is better technically is not overwhelmingly important. Both are capable of speeds in the hundreds of megabits per second in both directions over short distances.

Further, the relevant distances will be getting smaller as fiber is pulled closer and closer to the home by both cable and DSL carriers. Eventually fiber will go all the way into the home. Whoever manages to accomplish this, will then likely have a true natural monopoly, with the ability to increase the bandwidth of the connection at low cost. Victory in this race to bring fiber to the home will likely depend mostly on the strategies and tactics of the competing players, and not so much on technology.

The cell phone industry has been making capital expenditures of around $1,000 per subscriber, while copper or coax connections to add additional subscribers run about twice as high. In the financial markets, wireless carriers are valued at about $2,000 per subscriber. ILECs are valued at $2,000 to $3,000 per line, while cable TV networks are valued at $4,000 to $5,000 per subscriber.

In 1996, the US passed the Telecommunications Reform Act that was expected to create vigorous competition in all segments of communications. Six years later, after the telecom boom and bust, the entrenched ILECs appear to be even more securely entrenched, apparently the sole winners to emerge from all the turmoil. The reformers are beginning to concede that the "first mile" is a natural monopoly, and are being driven to consider remedies such as separating the ILECs into monopoly wholesale providers of basic network connectivity and retail service providers that alternative carriers might have a hope of competing with.

However, given the long lead times that US legislative and judicial systems operate on, especially where drastic changes are involved, there is very little hope of any such transformation being forced through in less than 5 years, and potentially it could take much longer. Even without any ILEC separation, though, we are likely to see several serious challenges to the ILEC monopoly emerge in the next half a dozen years.

The main challenge is likely to come from diversion of voice traffic to cell phones. Already a substantial fraction of the population regards cell phones as their primary communication tool, and that fraction is likely to increase. Policy makers who are interested in promoting competition could help this move along by forcing those ILECs that have not yet done so to completely sever their ties with cellular carriers. Competition from cellular carriers for voice is likely to force ILECs to concentrate on exploiting their natural advantage in bandwidth, and to emphasize Internet access. ILECs will also be forced to emphasize broadband by competition from cable TV companies.

For broadband communication, wireless distribution inside the house is especially attractive, given the costs of alternatives. Depending on how issues of scaling and business models are resolved, this approach could extend to a much wider communication network. So far wireless data communication has been a great disappointment, and 802.11 standards are the first ones that appear to be gaining wide acceptance. As wireless data spreads, and especially as voice transport capability is provided, we might see it offering serious competition to DSL and cable modem systems. What is especially attractive about wireless communication is that at least potentially it scales with the size of the population that is served, and so avoids the huge upfront costs of wireline infrastructure.

The traditional model for the telecom industry has been that of a carrier that provides all the equipment and systems and sells a service. This model has been fading for a long time, with customers buying their own phone sets, fax machines, and PBXs. A comparison with the computer industry is likely to be productive, especially since communication, information, and computation are becoming increasingly interrelated.

The general trend in the modern economy has been away from vertical integration and towards horizontal integration. This trend is consistent with what one would expect in view of Coase's theory of the firm, as improved communication makes it possible to use market mechanisms between different layers, and at the same time makes coordination easier.

Among the main advantages of a division into horizontal layers, with separate companies operating in each layer, is that it provides a method handling complexity and rapid change. It is worth noting that such separation was already visible inside the vertically integrated enterprises.

For example, in telecommunications, the wireline carriers have for quite a long time had essentially separate divisions handling the optical network and the voice and data networks that rode on top of it and were the only ones visible to most customers.

The computer industry is a prime example of the trend away from vertically integrated enterprises. A standard example of such an enterprise was IBM in the 1960s through much of the 1980s. It developed and produced its own processors, memories, hard disks, operating systems, application software, and so on. The current paradigm is that of horizontal players, in which Micron produces memory chips, Intel microprocessors,

Microsoft the operating system and basic applications, Dell assembles the components and sells them, etc. The most successful player in this game is Microsoft.

In the computer ındustry, everybody wants to be Microsoft, but there is only one Microsoft, and there cannot be too many Microsofts. Microsoft has annual revenues approaching $30 billion, after-tax profits approaching $12 billion, $38 billion in cash, and a stock market valuation of $330 billion. It has attained this enviable financial position by dominating the desktop software market, and appropriating the lion's share of the profits in PC software.

In communications, the trend towards a horizontal structure of the industry also appears inevitable. Who will adopt to it best is uncertain. The natural division would seem to be into providers of physical connectivity, providers of basic data transport, and outsourcers, who manage customer networks. The established long distance carriers, with their expertise in serving large enterprise customers, would seem to be best positioned to dominate in basic data transport and outsourcing. On the negative side, they have heavy debt loads and also the legacy of the consumer long distance business as a burden.

The ILECs have the financial resources to attempt moving into outsourcing, but lack the expertise, and would require a wrenching cultural change to adapt. Their natural niche seems to be in providing physical access and basic data transport, although even there, one could have separation into several layers.

Some parts of the telecom world appear destined for commoditization, especially long distance transport. The Internet at its core is a "stupid network," as David

Isenberg has called it. With technological progress and the fierce competition created by the massive overinvestment in that area, backbone transport is not and will not be all that big a piece of the telecom pie.

Local access is likely to be a large part of the industry. The costs are going to remain high, and economies of scale will limit competition. Hence revenues are going to be large, and profits are likely to be substantial. However, the potential for exorbitant profits will be slim, both because of regulation and growing competition. The greatest growth opportunities in telecommunications are likely to lie in services. As was mentioned above, the "stupid network" metaphor for the Internet ignores the huge costs at the edges of the network, costs that are often not explicit, since they involve time and aggravation for the customers. This again mirrors what happened in the computer industry.

It again brings up the example of IBM, a company that is in the process of transforming itself from a vertically integrated producer of computer systems to a service company, running other companies' IT operations. IBM has about three times the revenues of Microsoft, two thirds of the profits, a lower growth rate, and a stock market valuation about 55% that of Microsoft. However, it is regarded as a remarkable success story, and its stock price has not been devastated to the extent that shares of most of the other computer companies have been.

Definitions of Cyber-terms

The terms Internet, electronic commerce, electronic business, and cybertrade are used often. However, they are used interchangeably and with no common understanding of their scope or relationships. Establishing terms that clearly and consistently describe the growing and dynamic networked economy is a critical first step toward developing useful statistics about it. The definitions are used for the electronic revolution taking place in the economy, and must recognize that these changes take place in a larger economic context. For example, global competition, interest rates, laws and regulations, social concerns, industry traditions, and consumer preferences are all part of the broader "environment" which can affect all business activities.

Similarly, electronic and non-electronic businesses share an infrastructure of available economic resources, including natural resources, utilities, structures, equipment, telecommunication and other services, employees, and workforce skills. It is useful to think of the electronic economy as having three primary components—supporting infrastructure, electronic business processes, and electronic commerce transactions.

A common feature of both electronic business processes and electronic commerce transactions is reliance on the use of computer-mediated networks. It is reliance on the use of computer networks, and the benefits this can provide, that is the "bottom line" difference between electronic and other kinds of business.

There are three primary components of US electronic economy, and the feature shared by two of them, are defined below. Each definition includes examples of its scope and content. The definitions are intentionally broad to provide an inclusive framework for planning statistical measures, and to allow flexibility to incorporate continuing changes in the electronic economy.

E-business infrastructure

E-business infrastructure is the share of total economic infrastructure used to support electronic business processes and conduct electronic commerce transactions. It includes hardware, software, telecommunication networks, support services, and human capital used in electronic business and commerce. Examples of e-business infrastructure are:

— Computers, routers, and other hardware

— Satellite, wire, and optical communications and network channels

— System and applications software

— Support services, such as web site development and hosting, consulting, electronic payment, and certification services.

— Human capital, such as programmers.

Electronic business

Electronic business is any process that a business organization conducts over a computer-mediated network. Business organizations include any for-profit, governmental, or nonprofit entity. Their processes include production-, customer-, and internal or management-focused business processes. Examples of electronic business processes are:

— *Production*: focused processes include procurement, ordering, automated stock replenishment, payment processing and other electronic links with suppliers, as well as production control and processes more directly related to the production process.

— *Customer*: focused processes include marketing, electronic selling, processing of customers orders and payments, and customer management and support

— *Internal or management*: focused processes include automated employee services, training, information sharing, video conferencing, and recruiting.

Electronic commerce

Electronic commerce is any transaction completed over a computer-mediated network that involves the transfer of ownership or rights to use goods or services. Transactions occur within selected e-business processes and are "completed" when agreement is reached between the buyer and seller to transfer the ownership or rights to use goods or services. Completed transactions may have a zero price.

Computer-mediated networks

Computer-mediated networks are electronically linked devices that communicate interactively over network channels. Generally, both electronic devices will be computer-enabled, but at a minimum at least one device must be computer-enabled as in the case of a typical telephone linking with an computer-enabled interactive telephone system.

Typically, the interactive link involves minimal human intervention though someone activates the electronic devices, accesses the network, and may even assist with the process or transaction. For example, many e-commerce businesses are providing shoppers with the on-line capability of "chatting" with customer support representatives or even speaking with them through the use of internet telephony software. Examples of devices and networks are:

— Linked electronic devices such as computers, personal digital assistants, webTV,

— Internet-enabled cellular phones, and telephones linked with interactive telephone systems.

— Networks such as the Internet, intranets, extranets, Electronic Data Interchange (EDI) networks, and telecommunication networks. Networks may be either open or closed.

E-commerce transactions

Following are the examples of e-commerce transactions are:

— An individual purchases a book on the Internet.

— A government employee reserves a hotel room over the Internet.

— A business calls a toll free number and orders a computer using the seller's interactive telephone system.

— A business buys office supplies on-line or through an electronic auction.

— A retailer orders merchandise using an EDI network or a supplier's extranet.

— A manufacturing plant orders electronic components from another plant within the company using the company's intranet.

— An individual withdraws funds from an automatic teller machine (ATM).

Identifying e-commerce transactions often is not as straight forward as the previous examples may make it appear. An e-commerce transaction since agreement occurred over computer-mediated networks. In contrast, the purchase of a pre-packaged music CD from a computerized kiosk would not be considered an e-commerce transaction. Identifying and measuring e-commerce transactions is new for statistical agencies and it can be complicated. The simple example of an on-line retail book purchase illustrates some of these complexities and points out some of the measurement issues that remain to be addressed.

While comprehensive measures of e-commerce may be wanted to profile all of these transactions, such detailed business statistics coverage would be unprecedented. In addition, the value of e-commerce transactions, like their brick and mortar counterparts, are aggregated and presented by the industry of the business entity selling the goods or services so the industry classification system will impose additional measurement constraints.

For example, Bigbook would be classified in North American Industry Classification System (NAICS) retail industry 454110, Electronic Shopping and Mail-Order Houses along with traditional catalog stores. Data on employment, total sales, or e-commerce sales would be provided for the industry as whole; information would not be broken out between electronic shopping and mail order houses. Understanding the industry classification system and its implications for e-commerce and e-business measures is a must for all prospective data users. Moreover, classifying emerging and rapidly evolving businesses engaged in e-commerce activities will remain a challenge for statistical agencies. An additional complexity is that the transactions relating to John Doe's simple book purchase involve many parties and some play multiple roles.

The business-to-consumer transaction will involve a larger number of related business-to-business transactions. This transactions multiplier effect is not unique to e-business; however, its expected growth and continued change will add to the challenge of measuring e-business and e-commerce. Growth in transactions is expected because as e-commerce expands related business-to-business transactions will become more fragmented; participants will concentrate on performing their highest valued-activities and rely increasingly on third parties for lower-value added activities.

The measurement challenges of this growth include accounting for the increased volumes, identifying the new e-business players, maintaining up-to-date information for the known players, and avoiding double counting the value of related transactions. Change in the scope and nature of e-commerce transactions is expected because electronic business methods permit the players to change their roles relatively easily and they increasingly will do so. Examples of changes in roles are today seen in manufacturers and wholesalers who now sell directly to consumers, and in the "virtual" integration of firms through informal alliances that link firms electronically.

These new arrangements impose additional measurement challenges including identifying the new players and their roles, maintaining up-to-date information on them and how their roles are changing, and updating data collection methods. E-business is any process that a business organization conducts over a computer-mediated network. E-commerce is any transaction completed over a computer-mediated network that involves the transfer of ownership or rights to use goods or services. The definition includes both monetary and non monetary transactions.

Some transactions may have a zero price (for example, the download of free software) while other transactions may be paid in-kind or through barter. E-business infrastructure is the share of total economic infrastructure used to support processes and conduct e-commerce transactions. The definition includes hardware, software, telecommunication networks, support services, and human capital along with associated examples.

Network channels

Network channels include the Internet, intranets within organizations, extranets and Electronic Data Interchange networks linking trading partners, and telecommunication networks. Electronic linked devices include computers, personal digital assistants, webTV, Internet-enabled phones, and interactive telephone systems.

While the e-commerce examples also include a computer-enabled kiosk and an ATM as linked electronic devices, in the definition people have chosen to go with a short, rather than a long list of electronic devices to minimize possible reporting confusion. Fax machines, while clearly electronic devices that can link over network channels, were excluded because they do not communicate interactively.

Electronic gas pumps often are linked interactively over network channels with other electronic devices. The device, the electronic pump, can be activated in a number of different ways. ATM machine or a computer-enabled kiosk, once the device is activated the consumer can specify the transaction and complete the transaction.

The electronic pumps also support a number of E-business processes including tracking sales and gallons sold, with links to automated inventory replenishment systems to name a few. The functionality embedded in pumps is expected to grow. For example, BP Amoco PLC is planning to introduce even more sophisticated pumps that will include Web browsers and Windows CE operating system that will even permit the gas purchaser to order fast food at the pump.

Communication Revolution through E-mail

E-mail is the most important, unique method for communicating and developing relationships. It is easy to use. People also find it familiar and safe because it is similar in many respects to writing letters - minus the annoyances of addressing envelopes, licking stamps, and trips to the mail box. Of all the methods for developing relationships on the internet, it is the most common - and perhaps the most powerful. Although friendships and romances may indeed begin in text-driven chat rooms, MOOs, MUDs, or the newer multimedia chat environments, these relationships almost always progress to e-mail as a way to deepen the communication. It is a more private, more reliable, less chaotic way to talk.

Even when other methods improve greatly by becoming more effectively visual and auditory - as in video teleconferencing - e-mail will not disappear. Many people will prefer it BECAUSE it is a non-visual and non-auditory form of communication. After all, we don't see people rushing out to buy video equipment to accessorize their telephone - even though that technology has been available for some time. E-mail is not just electronic mail sent via the internet. E-mail communication creates a psychological space in which pairs of people - or groups of people - interact.

People type words to communicate via e-mail. More technologically sophisticated methods enable you to incorporate pictures and sounds into the message, but that's a more complicated process that destroys the simplicity and ease of use that attracts many people to e-mailing. On the other hand, some people may not be attracted to e-mail BECAUSE it involves typing.

While everyone knows how to talk, not everyone knows how to type. Some people also may not feel comfortable or skilled in expressing themselves through writing. The typing/writing barrier filters some people out of the e-mail world. For those who love to write, e-mail is heaven.

In the typed text of e-mail, you can't see other people's faces or hear them speak. All those subtle voice and body language cues are lost, which can make the nuances of communicating more difficult. But humans are creative beings. Avid e-mailers have developed all sorts of innovative strategies for expressing themselves through typed text.

A skilled writer may be able to communicate considerable depth and subtlety in the deceptively simple written word. Despite the lack of face-to-face cues, conversing via e-mail has evolved into a sophisticated, expressive art form. People may not know who you are or where you are when you send them an e-mail. If you want, you can use a pseudonym in the message. And the return address contains only general information about where you are. The average user doesn't know how to track down the origin and identity of a mysterious message.

If someone is determined to remain hidden, they can send their mail through an anonymous mailer service that will strip away all identifying information from the e-mail. This potential for anonymity in e-mailing disinhibits some people. They say things they wouldn't ordinarily say. The lack of face-to-face cues amplifies this disinhibiting effect. In some cases the result may be people who speak in an aggressive, antisocial manner. Sometimes it encourages people to be more open, honest, and affectionate. Anonymity isn't intrinsically a "good" or "bad" thing. It cuts both ways. E-mail conversations do not occur in "real time." You and your partner do not have to be sitting at the computer at the same moment in order to talk.

Unlike face-to-face encounters, which are synchronous, e-mail discussions do not require you to respond on-the-spot to what they other has said. You have time to think, evaluate, and compose your reply. Some people take advantage of this convenient "zone for reflection." Some do not. Because e-mail communication is asynchronous, the rate at which you converse is maneuverable. A conversation may occur over the course of minutes, days, weeks, or months. Interactive time can be shortened or stretched, as needed. Changes in the pacing of the e-mail exchange between two people reflects the dynamics of their relationship.

Most e-mail programs allow you to cc people or create a mailing list. These features make it very easy to expand a dyad conversation into a group discussion. Large groups of dozens or more people can be managed through such programs as "listserv." The membership boundary of the e-mail interactive space is as flexible as its members want it to be. Sometimes the boundaries are hidden: people can be dropped from a discussion without their even knowing it.

Spam - Inevitably, e-mail users are subjected to the "spam" of unrequested messages designed to sell an idea or a product. Junk mail. To internet oldtimers, spam is anathema. It's the apocalyptic sign of the commercialization of cyberspace. People subjectively experience e-mail as a personal space in which they interact with friends and colleagues. Spam is the commercial that pops up in your face, intruding on that private zone.

In the list of incoming mail, it stands out like a wart. One of the very few good things about spam is that it reminds you of how e-mail is NOT a totally private space. Unwelcomed others can inject their irrelevance. And although it rarely happens, technically clever sociopathic and other nosy people can secretly listen in on your conversations.

Today, almost everyone is using e-mail, not everyone is using it to the same extent. One way to classify people is by the frequency and intensity of their e-mail use. People in each category tend to behave a bit differently in their e-mail relationships than people in other categories.

The impact e-mail has on your interpersonal life increases as you become more avidly involved. It becomes an upward spiraling process: the more you e-mail, the more relationships you develop, the more you need to continue e-mailing in order to stay connected to your colleagues and friends. With that ever-expanding e-mail life comes increased skill in composing and reading e-mail.

You become sensitized to the nuances of e-mail relationships, which makes that interpersonal world even more enticing, challenging, and rewarding. For avid e-mail users, the computer is a major feature of their interpersonal and/or professional life, including dyad relationships and group memberships. Their online world has become deeply ingrained into their psyche and e-mail is an extremely important pathway for psychologically maintaining the integrity of that world.

They check their e-mail at least once a day, often several times a day. It's one of very first things they do in the morning and may be the last thing they do before bedtime. E-mailmay receive a hundred or more messages - the bulk of those messages coming from the group lists to which they belong.

Some avid users may have their e-mail programs set to automatically download at regular intervals, while even more hardcore users check each message as soon as it comes in. For the avid user, a technical failure resulting in a loss of e-mail capability is a catastrophe. You feel cut off, out of the loop.

Many avid users have some type of back-up system to counteract such disasters - for example, a second or third e-mail account, or a second e-mail capable computer (e.g., a computer at the office and at home). Avid users almost always have at least one online buddy who acts as an emergency intermediary. When the user's e-mail capability goes down, he or she contacts the buddy who relays news of the user's predicament to their online friends and colleagues. Regular e-mail users check and write e-mail a few times each week, often at at a prescribed time.

Their internet relationships can become a very significant feature of their lives, as with the avid user - although their e-mail worlds do not take on the same intensity as with avid users. Technical failures resulting in disconnection also doesn't stir up the same degree of anxiety. The casual e-mail user does e-mail sporadically, maybe once a week, or less than that. For these users, e-mail is a curiosity, a toy to play with, an amusement for leisure time. They may enjoy tinkering with this form of communication - and may even establish some friends and colleagues through it.

But e-mail has not become an important feature of their interpersonal world. Difficulties may arise when regular users - and especially avid users - begin e-mailing with casual users. There is a disparity in the perceived importance of developing the relationship via e-mail. The avid or regular user may be expecting more frequent exchanges, but does not receive them. Experienced users quickly recognize this disparity and adjust accordingly. E-mail usually is one of the first things a new internet user attempts. So the newbie e-mail user usually has just entered the world of cyberspace They don't understand the rules of the road or how things work. They may breach etiquette, like typing in caps, which is the text-talk equivalent of shouting. They don't fully understand the depth and complexity of the e-mail world. They don't yet appreciate its potential for developing relationships. Essentially, they don't know what they are getting into.

Avid users often can spot a newbie very quickly. Some of these more experienced users enjoy taking the newbie under their wing. Other undesirable types may toy with or try to take advantage of the naive newbie.

A person's ability to communicate effectively via e-mail depends highly on his or her writing skills. People who hate to write probably will not become consistent e-mail users. Regular and avid users usually enjoy writing. Some even report that they PREFER writing as a way to express themselves. They take delight in words, sentence structure, and the opportunity to craft exactly how they wish to express their thoughts and moods.

They enjoy that "zone of reflection" where they can ponder and self-reflect before expressing themselves. As such, e-mail usually is a less spontaneous form of communicating than speech. Unlike verbal conversation - where words issue forth and immediately evaporate - writing places one's thoughts in a more visible, permanent, concrete, and objective format. An e-mail message is a tiny packet of self-representation that is launched off into cyberspace. Some even experience it as a creative work, a gift sent to one's internet pal. It's a piece of oneself that experienced e-mail users enjoy constructing. The quality of the relationship between e-mail correspondents rests on their writing skills. The better people can express themselves through writing, the more the relationship can develop and deepen.

Poor writing can result in misunderstandings and possibly conflicts. In the absence of an accurate perception of what the other is trying to say, people tend to project their own expectations, anxieties, and fantasies onto the other. A disparity in writing ability between e-mail partners also can be problematic. The equivalent in in-person encounters would be one person who is very eloquent and forthcoming, talking to another who speaks awkwardly and minimally.

The loquacious one eventually may resent putting so much effort into the relationship and taking all the risks of self-disclosure. The quiet one may feel controlled, ignored, and misunderstood. We tend to think of writing abilities as a fixed skill - a tool for expressing oneself that is either sophisticated or not. It's also possible that the quality of one's writing is affected by the quality of the relationship with the other.

As an e-mail relationship deepens - and trust develops - a person may open up to more expressive forms of writing. They are more willing to experiment, take risks - not just in what specific thoughts or emotions they express, but also in the words and composition used. Spelling and grammar conjure up all sorts of memories and emotions from the school years of one's childhood. Your self-concept may ride on those memories. In the course of an e-mail relationship, those issues from the past may be stirred up. Writing isn't just a tool for developing the e-mail relationship.

Writing affects the relationship, and the relationship influences the quality of the writing. Writing effectiveness changes as a result of what is happening in the ongoing e-mail encounter. Composition advances when people feel safe and are ready to explore; it regresses when they feel threatened, hurt, or angry. Those changes reflect the developmental changes in the relationship. In addition to writing skill, writing STYLE also affects the e-mail relationship and is in turn affected by it. Concrete, emotional and abstract expression, complexity of vocabulary and sentence structure, the organization and flow of thought - all reflect one's cognitive/personality style and influence how the other reacts to you.

Compulsive people may construct highly organized, intellectualized messages with little emotional revelation. Histrionic people may show less concern about organization and much more for the emotions they express. Narcissists may write extremely long, rambling blocks of paragraphs. Schizoids may produce very short but penetrating messages. Different writing/personality styles may be compatible, incompatible, or complementary to other styles.

There are seven components for E-mail messages:

(1) the sender's name as indicated in your incoming mailbox,

(2) the subject line, as indicated in your incoming mailbox,

(3) the greeting that introduces the body of the message,

(4) the body of message, including quoted text,

(5) the sign-off line and name, and,

(6) the signature block. The body of the message is what most people consider the actual "message" itself.

However, the other components of the message also can be tiny gems of communication. Much meaning can be packed into those little nuggets. How those deceptively simple components of the message change over time may signal important changes in the relationship.

The Sender's Name reflects the ongoing identity that one wishes to present online. The name chosen usually is one's real name, a pseudonym, or a combined name.

Using one's real name indicates a wish to simply be oneself. It's a straightforward, "honest" presentation. Pseudonyms are more mysterious, playful approaches. "Can you guess who I am?" They express some hidden aspect of the person's self-concept. They reveal unconscious motivating fantasies and wishes about one's identity.

A combined name is a "letting it be known" that you have a partner - that the two of you are sharing the e-mail program and may BOTH be reading all the mail. When people change the username setting in their e-mail program, it reflects an important change in how they wish to present their ongoing, online identity. Moving from a pseudonym to one's real name expresses the wish to drop the "mask". Changing the combined name to a single name is a move towards separation and individuation that invites more private, one-on-one dialogue.

The subject line is a tiny microcosm unto itself. Most often it's used to simply summarize or introduce the major idea/s contained in the body of the message. But experienced e-mail users understand the more subtle techniques for communicating meaning and emotion in the titles they bestow to their e-mail. The subject line can lead into, highlight, or elaborate a particular idea in the message. It can ask a definitive question, shoot back a definitive answer, joke, tease, prod, berate, shout, whisper, or emote.

Sometimes it's meaning may blatantly or discreetly contradict the sentiment expressed in the body of the message. A creative application of caps, commas, slashes, parentheses, and other keyboard characters adds emphasis and complexity to the thoughts and emotions expressed in the subject line. In an e-mail archive, examining the list of subject lines across the development of the relationship is like perusing the headlines of a newspaper over the course of months or years.

It reflects the flow of important themes in the history of the e-mail encounter. These patterns or trends over time might reveal hidden or unconscious elements in relationship between the two people. For example, one interesting feature is the use of "re:" as a prefix to the subject line. The use of "re:" versus creating a new subject line can be an interesting dynamic interchange between e-mail partners. Creating a new line is a bit like taking the lead in the relationship by introducing a new title for the interaction - like creating a headline for the little "story" that is the ongoing dialogue. It's an attempt to conceptualize, summarize, and highlight what the person perceives as the most important feature of the conversation.

Creating a new subject line calls into play the "observing ego" - that ability to step back and reflect on what is happening. It shows a sense of responsibility and ownership for the dialogue - in some cases maybe even an attempt to control the dialogue. In this fashion, some e-mail partners "duel" with each other via the subject line. Simply clicking on reply without creating a new message title may indicate less of an observing ego and more of a spontaneous reaction. Some people chronically fail to create a new subject line and persistently use "re:" They may be a bit passive in the relationship, or lazy. They may not feel that sense of responsibility, ownership, or control. If this isn't true, their partner may still perceive them as being that way. Spammers will try to exploit the dynamics of a subject line in order to trick you into opening the message.

Beware of subject headings written all in caps, embellished with asterisks and exclamation points, or containing overly friendly or seductive messages—especially when you don't recognize the sender's name. If it looks and smells like spam, it's spam.

Similar to writing letters or meeting someone on the street, the conversation usually begins with a greeting of some sort. Different greetings convey slightly different emotional tones and levels of intimacy. It sets the mood for the rest of the message. Over the course of a batch of messages, the back-and-forth changes in the greeting can become a revealing little dance - sometimes playful, sometimes competitive. No greeting at all is an interesting phenomenon that cuts both ways.

In some cases, it may reveal that the sender is lazy, passive, or how he/she lacks any personal connection to you. In an ongoing, back-and-forth dialogue, there may be no greetings at all throughout a string of exchanged e-mails. In the face-to-face world, you don't say "hello" in the midst of a energetic discussion. In cyberspace, the same principle holds. Although each e-mail message LOOKS like a letter that traditionally starts off with a greeting, it actually isn't. It's a segment of an ongoing conversation. The body of the message is the most complex component of the e-mail.

Messages can vary widely in length, organization, the flow of ideas, the use of quoted text, spelling errors, grammar sophistication, the use of caps, tabs, smileys and other unique keyboard characters, the spacing of paragraphs, and the overall visual "feel" of the message. The structure of the e-mail body reflects the cognitive and personality style of the individual who creates it. People who are compulsive may strive for well organized and logically constructed messages with few, if any, spelling or grammatical errors.

Those with a histrionic flair may offer a more dramatic presentation, where neatness plays a back seat to the expressive use of spacing, caps, unique keyboard characters, and colorful language. People with schizoid tendencies may be pithy, while those who are more impulsive may dash off a disorganized, spelling-challenged message with emotional phrases highlighted in shouted caps.

Empathic people will specifically respond to what their e-mail partners have said. They ask their partners questions about themselves and their lives. But they also construct their messages anticipating what it will be like for the recipient to read it. They write in a style that is both engaging and readily understood. With appropriate use of spacing, paragraph breaks, and various keyboard characters to serve as highlights and dividers, they visually construct the message so that it is easy and pleasing to read. Essentially, they are good writers who pay attention to the needs of their audience. This is quite unlike people with narcissistic tendencies, who have difficulty putting themselves into the shoes of the recipient. They may produce lengthy blocks of unbroken text, expecting that their partner will sustain an interest in scrolling, reading, scrolling, reading, for seemingly endless screens of long-winded descriptions of what the sender thinks and feels.

Paradoxically, the narcissistic person's need to be heard and admired may result in the recipient hitting the delete key out of boredom. A carefully, empathically constructed e-mail sometimes can lack spontaneity. It is possible to over-think and micro-manage the message to the point where it sounds a bit contrived. Perhaps the most effective message is one that strikes a balance between spontaneity and carefully planned organization. Also, short messages with some obvious spelling errors, glitches, or a slightly chaotic visual appearance can be a sincere expression of affection and friendship - as if the person is willing to let you see how they look hanging around the house, wearing an old t-shirt and jeans. Or such a message can be a genuine expression of the person's state of mind at that moment. In the course of an ongoing e-mail relationship, there will be a engaging rhythm of spontaneous and carefully thought out messages that parallels the ebb and flow of the relationship itself.

Experienced e-mailers have developed a variety of keyboard techniques to overcome some of the limitations of typed text - techniques that almost lend a vocal and kinesthetic quality to the message. They attempt to make e-mail conversations less like postal letters and more like a face-to-face encounter. Thoughts and feelings placed in parentheses or brackets are a kind of subvocal muttering to oneself - as if one is thinking outloud, tipping one's hand, allowing the other to peek inside one's head. There's an honest or even vulnerable quality to this parenthetical expression because you're letting the other person in on something that otherwise could be kept hidden.

Actions placed in parentheses indicate body language - an attempt to convey some of the face-to-face cues that are missing in typed text encounters. Options range from a simple standard grin [g] to more complex, personally tailored descriptions. Of course, people have much more conscious control over these parenthetical actions than they do over body language in the in-person world. Voice accentuation can be accomplished using caps, asterisks, underlining, and other keyboard characters. Exclamation points add to the effect. It's an attempt to mimic the changes in voice emphasis that you might hear in face-to-face world as well as the emotions that accompany that emphasis.

A series of dots - "trailers" - can be used creatively in a variety of ways. Usually they mimic a pause in one's speaking. That pause might be used dramatically, to lead the person into or psychologically prepare them for your next idea - sometimes even a "you might want to sit down for this" warning. Or the trailer indicates a pause to breath, a transition in your thinking, or a temporary lapse or faltering in your train of thought. The addition of the "um" and "uh" in that last example helps simulate the sense of hesitation and confusion in that faltering thought process. As the term "emoticons" suggests, these keyboard faces are tagged onto the end of a sentence to enhance emotional expression. Including the smiley, the frown, and the winky, they may amplify the feeling expressed in the sentence, add a subtle affective spin to the sentence, or even contradict its sentiment. The smiley often is used to clarify a friendly feeling when otherwise the tone of your sentence might be ambiguous. It also can reflect benign assertiveness, an attempt to undo hostility, subtle denial or sarcasm, self-consciousness, and apologetic anxiety. The winky is like elbowing your e-mail partner, implying that you both know something that doesn't need to be said outloud.

The ubiquitous LOL (laughing out loud) - which originated in chat rooms - is very handy tool for responding to something funny without having to actually say "Oh, that's funny!" It's feels more natural and spontaneous - more like the way you would respond in a face-to-face situation. The sequence of acronyms listed above indicate increasing levels of mirth - beginning with the weak, perhaps even perfunctory "lol" and moving toward the unrestrained "rolling on floor laughing" and raucous "laughing my ass off."

How and when to use exclamation points is a bit of an art form. Unless the sentiment of the sentence is clearly negative, they tend to lighten up the mood. But like spice in cooking, there are dangers of excess as well as omissions. Leaving out exclamation points entirely - as in the first example above - may result in a message that appears bland or ambiguous.

Without even a hint of enthusiasm, some people might wonder if the sender is suppressing some hostility. On the other extreme, too many exclamation points - as in the third example above - may result in a message mood that seems contrived, shallow, or even uncomfortably manic. A message peppered lightly with exclamations, at just the right spots, can give the message a varying texture of energy that emphasizes what needs to be emphasized.

An advantage of e-mail conversations over face-to-face ones is that you have the ability to quote parts or all of what your partner said in his previous message. Hitting "reply" and then tacking your response to the top or bottom of the e-mail is a quick and easy rejoinder. In some cases it's a very appropriate strategy - especially when your partner's message was short, which makes it obvious what you are replying to. However, inserting a reply at the top or bottom of an entire quoted message which is LONG may be perceived by your partner as laziness or indifference on your part - as if you simply hit the reply button, typed your response, and clicked on "send." The person may not be sure exactly what part of the message you are responding to. You also force your partner to download an unnecessarily long file. Sticking a reply at the end of the lengthy quoted message can be particularly annoying because it forces the person to scroll and scroll and scroll, looking for the reply.

The alternative to quoting the whole message is to select out and respond individually to SEGMENTS of it. The arrow marks may appear at the beginning of each line of quoted text, or the sender may place them a the beginning and end of the quoted segment.

Some people use [snip] to indicate that what follows is quoted text. It takes more time and effort to quote segments rather than the whole message, but there are several advantages. People may appreciate the fact that you put that time and effort into your response. It makes your message clearer, more to the point, easier to read. It may convey to your partner a kind of empathic attentiveness because you are responding to specific things that she said. You are letting the person know exactly what from their message stood out in your mind. Replying to several segments can result in an entertaining and intriguingly rich e-mail in which there are several threads of conversation occurring at the same time, each with a different content and emotional tone.

In one multilevel e-mail, you may be joking, explaining, questioning, recalling a past event, and anticipating a future one. For continuity and clarity, several back-and-forth exchanges can be captured by embedding quoted segments. There is a downside to quoting segments. In flame wars, you often see people citing more and more of what the opponent said, using it as ammunition to launch counterattacks.

A contrast between the greeting and the sign-off may be significant - as if writing the e-mail altered the person's attitudes and feelings. Across a series of messages, the sign-off lines may be a string of repartees between the partners that amplifies, highlights or adds nuance to their dialogue in the message bodies. The progression of exchanged sign-off lines may itself become an encapsulated, Morse-code dialogue between the partners. "Sincerely," "Regards" or other similar sign-offs are rather safe, all-purpose tools borrowed from the world of postal mail. They are formal, polite ways to exit. Some avid e-mailer users use them sparingly because they suggest a snail-mail mentality and a lack of appreciation for the creatively conversational quality of e-mail. Almost invariably, the sender's name follows the sign-off line. Simply typing your real name is the easiest, most straightforward tactic. If the e-mail partners both belong to the same online community, they may have to make a conscious choice about whether to use their real names or their online usernames. The online name can be entertaining and revealing, but changing from that imaginary handle to your real name may be a gesture of honestly and intimacy - a kind of "coming out."

Creatively playing with your sign-off name can be an another effective way to express your state of mind, some aspect of your identity, or your relationship to your e-mail partner. Usually this type of play only feels appropriate with friends, or it indicates that one wishes to be friendly, loose, and imaginative. Proclaiming their identification with net culture, people sometimes apply the common cyberspace practice of fusing two capitalized words to create a "neologistic name" for themselves. Leaving out the sign-off line and/or name may be an omission with meaning. It might suggest a curt, efficient, formal, impersonal, or even angry attitude about the conversation.

The ending could appear especially bureaucratic or impersonal if the person inserts his signature block and nothing else. On the other hand, friends may leave out a sign-off line and name as a gesture of informality and familiarity. "You know it's me." They may assume that the conversation is ongoing - as in a face-to-face talk - so there's no need to type anything that suggests a good-bye. Many e-mail programs offer the option of creating a signature file or "block" that automatically will be placed at the bottom of your message.

People usually place factual or identifying information into that file - such as their full name, title, e-mail address, postal address, institutional affiliation, phone number, etc. It's a prepackaged stamp indicating "who and where I am." What a person puts into that file reflects what they hold dear to their public identity. Some programs offer the feature of writing alternative signature files, which gives the person the opportunity to create several different fingerprints—each one tailored for a specific purpose. For example, one may be formal and factual, another more casual and playful. Each one is a slightly different slice of the person's identity. Because all signature blocks have a non-spontaneous, "prepackaged" feeling to them, friends often make a conscious effort to turn it off when writing to a cyberspace pal. In a sense, you are dropping your status and title while also assuming the person knows your e-mail address, phone number, etc.

The message in which the sig block is first dropped probably reflects the sender's move towards feeling more friendly and casual in the relationship. As with the sign-off line and name, a change in a person's sig block reflects a shift in their identity or in how they wish to present their identity.

Like any subculture, the world of e-mailing has developed a unique language. Having its own novel terms and expressions that outsiders don't understand gives any group a sense of distinctive identity. To be in the group is to be in the know. If you appropriately use the parlance, you are demonstrating your knowledge of and belonging to the subculture. The unique language also evolves for purely practical reasons. It makes communication more efficient.

In the world of avid e-mail users, a variety of acronyms and abbreviations have developed. Many of these were borrowed from chat lingo. A private language also may develop between two people or among a small group of people who e-mail each other frequently.

It may include unique acronyms, expressions, character symbols and words (neologisms) that only those people understand. The evolution of that private language reflects the evolving identity, cohesion, and intimacy of the dyad or group. Usually the language crystallizes around issues that are discussed frequently and therefore personally important to the e-mail partners.

Because e-mail has an adjustable conversing speed, the pacing of message exchanges will vary over the course of an e-mail relationship. The excitement of getting to know each other - and enjoying each others company - will result in an increasing pace that eventually plateaus into a rate of exchange that feels comfortable to both partners. As a general rule, the more frequently people e-mail each other, the more important and intimate the relationship feels to them.

Some people e-mail each other every day, or several times a day. Bursts in the intensity of the pace occur when "hot" topics are being discussed, when recent events in one's life need to be explained, or when work needs to be done. These bursts may reflect a sudden deepening of the intimacy in the relationship.

Declines in the pace may indicate a temporary or longterm weakening of the bonds between the couple - either due to a growing disinterest in the relationship or distractions from other sectors of one's life. Significant changes in the cadence always indicates a significant change in feelings, attitudes, or commitment. When people become enthused about e-mail, they may expect that their partners will respond at a pace as intense as their own enthusiasm. They may even unconsciously experience the interaction as if it is a face-to-face encounter - and so, perhaps unconsciously, they are expecting an almost immediate reply. Experienced e-mail users understand that different people have different paces. Some do e-mail every day; some two or three times a week; some once a week or less. Even avid and regular users have slightly different rhythms. You adjust yourself accordingly. You settle into a tempo that is right for each relationship. You accept that tempo as a meaningful indication of what that relationship is about. Drastic drops in the pace, or an apparent failure of the partner to respond at all, throws you into the "black hole" experience.

The partner's silence may be a sign of anger, indifference, stubborn withdrawal, punishment, laziness, preoccupation with other things... But you don't know for sure. The ambiguity inherent in the no-reply easily can become a blank screen onto which we project our own expectations, emotions, and anxieties.

Without hearing a person's voice - or seeing body language and facial expressions - you may not be exactly sure what the person means. This ambiguity enhances the tendency to project your own expectations, wishes, and anxieties unto the somewhat shadowy figure sitting at the other end of the internet - what is called a "transference reaction."

As an e-mail relationship develops over time, there may be ebbs and flows in the transferential feelings and attitudes towards the other person. When you first connect through e-mail, they tend to be minimal since you do not know the other person and have little psychological investment in the relationship.

Transference reactions are more likely to surface when emotional attachments begin to form but you still do not have a good "feel" for the person due to that lack of f2f cues. Other peak moments occur when emotional topics come up but you are unable to pinpoint exactly where the other person stands on the issue. Under ideal conditions, as we spend more and more time conversing with an e-mail partner, we begin to understand and work through those transference reactions so that we can see the other person as he/she really is.

However, even under the best of circumstances, there often is some aspect of our mental image of the other person that is based more on our own expectations and needs than on the reality of the other person. It may be the way we think he looks, her voice sounds, or some aspect of his personality. We may not even be consciously aware that we've formed that impression until we meet the person f2f and discover, much to our surprise, that they are - in some way - very different than what we expected.

Generally speaking, transference reactions are unconscious. We don't see them coming, and don't fully realize how they are steering our behavior. That's why they can get lead us astray and into trouble. Some incoming e-mail may be prepackaged with transference even though the person is a complete stranger to us. If you have a web site - or other information about you is available on the internet - people can form inaccurate impressions which they launch your way in the form of an e-mail. They may idealize you, detest you, or anything inbetween.

These kind of transference reactions often are deeply ingrained, prepared responses in the person that are ready to leap out at any opportune moment. Leaning towards passive dependency, they are operating at a rather immature interpersonal level. They see others in terms of their own needs rather than as separate people with needs of their own. The spoon-feeder also might be a good example of transference towards one's computer that carries over into transference towards other people. Unfortunately, another common transference reaction is the "chip on my shoulder" e-mail.

People who have antagonistic conflicts with authority figures may feel free to send a flaming e-mail to someone they perceive as an parental figure. The sometimes extreme hostility in such a message reflects the depth and intensity of the transference reaction. Anyone who has a web site that in any way presents themselves as an authority on some topic may be subjected to the "chip on my shoulder" e-mail.

A big advantage of e-mail encounters over f2f ones is that you can keep an exact record of what was said. At your leisure you can reread and reflect on the exchanges between you and your e-mail partner. If two people only know each other via e-mail - and at least one of them saves all of the exchanges messages - we could even make the argument that the "relationship" has been preserved in its entirety. Often, however, a person only saves some of the messages, probably those that are especially meaningful - emotional high points, moments of intimacy, important personal information, or other milestones in the relationship. Comparing the messages saved by one person to those saved by the partner could reveal similarities and discrepancies in what each of them finds most important about the relationship.

One person might savor humor, practical information, personal self-disclosures, emotional recoll-ections, or intellectual debate - while the other may not. Saving mostly one's own messages, or mostly the other person's messages, may reflect a difference in focus on either self or other. The area of significant overlap in saved messages reflects the common ground of interest and attitude that holds the relationship together. It's very possible that there might be a significant difference between partners in the number of saved messages. The person who saves less - or maybe none at all - may have a lower investment in the relationship. Or they may not be as self-reflective about relationships as people who wish to reread and think about what was said. On the other hand, that person may simply have less of a need to capture, preserve, or control the relationship.

There are several stages in the development of an e-mail relationship. First, the people must come in contact with each other. That may seem like a serendipitous or uneventful occurrence - they just "happened" to run into each other on the internet, or that first round of e-mail involved some "simple" request for information. But often there is more going on below the surface. Although, theoretically, people can connect with everyone else on the internet, they don't. They establish ongoing relationships with only a handful of people. Consciously - and often unconsciously - we filter through the hundreds and thousands of names that scroll down our monitor and select out those people that have similar interests to ours, those that address our psychological and emotional needs those that fit our transference dynamics. When reflecting on one of your ongoing e-mail relationships, it's interesting to open your archive and look up those first few messages that were exchanged. Those first few messages can reveal the needs and emotional dynamics that sparked the relationship. As in all relationships, the momentum begins with those sparked dynamics and evolves from there.

The people gradually reveal more about themselves to each other, which adds more layers of complexity onto the core dynamics that drew them together. The lack of face-to-face cues encourages them to discuss thoughts and feelings that they otherwise might not reveal - which helps solidify the bond between them. But filling in for that lack of face-to-face cues also deepens the relationship. Because cyberspace easily can be a world isolated from one's "real" life - a world where you can remain anonymous or take on an imaginative identity - revealing your ACTUAL identity is taken as a sign of intimacy and commitment. The more people start to share that kind of real-world information in their e-mail, the more the relationship is deepening. The developmental path in e-mail relationships is one that leads towards becoming more and more real to the other person. For the relationship to move beyond a certain point, the couple will want and need to have more real-time and face-to-face contact. They might try meeting in online chat, which can make the other person's "presence" seem more powerful and thereby enhance the feeling of actually "being together" in real time. It also tests each other's commitment to the relationship, because you both have to be there at a specific time. If they have the technical skills, they might try communicating with video or audio streaming. They might attach pictures of themselves to their e-mail.

An even bigger move forward is to step outside the sometimes invisible psychological boundary that "we are ONLINE friends." You break the cyberspace barrier by sending letters, photos, and gifts via postal mail.... or telephone the other person... or you take the final, inevitable step of actually meeting your friend in-person. Each of these moves towards becoming more real to the e-mail partner is a significant turning point in the relationship.

The thoughts and feelings that are discussed during and after each of these more intimate contacts builds new dimensions to the relationship. This is especially true of taking that big step forward by meeting your e-mail companion in-person. Both of you are taking that decisive step OUT of cyberspace and into the face-to-face encounter. It can be a bit anxiety-provoking. Some experienced online people feel they can suspend any expectations about what others will actually be like when they meet in-person. They claim that they are rarely surprised by that real world encounter. Others say that got to know someone so well through e-mail that meeting in person seemed very smooth and natural. In many cases, however, finally standing toe to toe with the other person can be a real eye-opener. The companion is not exactly what you expected. They look or talk differently than you had imagined. Some aspect of their personality is very different than you had imagined.

Due to the lack of f2f cues, people do not act the same in e-mail as they do in-person - and that difference may be striking when you meet. On the other hand, the contrast in how they appear on and offline may be the result of the false impression you had formed of them. Standing toe to toe, you have the opportunity to test out the image of your companion that you had created in your mind. You may have wanted or needed the person to be a certain way. Steered by your past intimate relationships, you may have EXPECTED them to be a certain way. Or you may have completely overlooked something in the e-mail that couldn't be ignored in the f2f encounter. Stated in a nutshell, meeting the person gives you the opportunity to understand and work through your transference reactions. Meeting in-person often will deepen the relationship. Afterwards the couple discuss, assimilate, reminisce, and cherish the encounter. They build on it. They share the ways in which the meeting confirmed and altered their perceptions of each other.

As such, ideally, they help each other understand and work through their transference reactions. But the in-person meeting doesn't always enhance the relationship. People may be disappointed after the meeting. The companion was not what they had hoped for. This unfortunate outcome may indicate that transference wishes were strong but off target. Some e-mail companions may not have the opportunity to meet each other. In some cases, the relationship still thrives - though there may be periods when the conversation dwindles. In other cases, the e-mail contact fades away for good. A face-to-face meeting may have been needed to energize the relationship, or perhaps it was inevitable that the relationship would evaporate. Some people choose NOT to phone or meet in-person their e-mail companion, even though such meetings could be arranged. They prefer to limit the relationship to cyberspace.

Perhaps they fear that their expectations and hopes will be dashed, or they feel more safe and comfortable with the relative anonymity of e-mail contact. They may be relishing the online fantasy they have created for themselves. Or they simply enjoy the e-mail relationship as it is and have no desire the develop the relationship any further. In all cases, choosing not to increase face-to-face contact with the e-mail partner is a choice not to make the relationship more intimate, well-rounded, or reality-based.

Experienced e-mailers often have friends and colleagues with whom they converse in-person and via e-mail on a regular basis. These dual relationships can be tricky. Sometimes the two realms become a bit dissociated from each other. The relationship starts to operate on two different psychological levels. Due to the lack of f2f cues in e-mail, thoughts and feelings that are difficult to express in-person may surface online. Those disclosures may occur consciously or unconsciously. Unless those disclosures are quickly brought into the f2f relationship, a gap starts to develop between the online encounters and the in-person meetings. It may become more and more difficult to speak in-person about what was said online.

The f2f relationship may become uncomfortable, or feel stiff and shallow. It's best to prevent this uneasy situation before it starts. Even under the most benign of circumstances, you may experience a tiny psychological hurdle that needs to be jumped in order to bring the online encounter into the f2f encounter, and vice versa. But do jump it. The most rewarding outcome is an integrated in-person and e-mail relationship. The beauty of e-mail is that you have the opportunity to contact people from around the world.

2

Internet: Learning to Live Together

The Internet has been growing at unprecedented rates. Because it is versatile and penetrates deeply into the economy, it is affecting all of society, and therefore has attracted inordinate amounts of public attention. The growth rates of the Internet into the proper context by providing comparisons with other communications services. The overwhelmingly predominant view has been that Internet traffic doubles every three or four months. Such unprecedented rates did prevail during the crucial two-year period of 1995 and 1996, when the Internet first burst onto the scene as a major new factor with the potential to transform the economy.

The Internet traffic is about doubling each year. The evidence was always plentiful, and the only thing lacking was the interest in investigating the question. By the year 2000, though, the myth of Internet traffic doubling every three or four months was getting hard to accept. Very simple arithmetic shows that such growth rates, had they been sustained throughout the period from 1995 to the end of 2000, would have produced absurdly high traffic volumes. For example, at the end of 1994, traffic on the NSFNet backbone, which was well instrumented, came to about 15 TB/month. Had just that traffic grown at 1,500% per year, by the end of 2000, there would have been about 250,000,000 TB/month of backbone traffic in the US. Assume 150 million Internet users in the U.S., that would produce a data flow of about 5 Mb/s for each user around the clock.

The assumption of a doubling of traffic every four months produces traffic volumes which are only slighly less absurd. Table 1 shows estimates for traffic on the Internet. The data for 1990 through 1994 is that for the NSFNet backbone, and so is very precise. It is incomplete only to the extent of neglecting what is thought to have been small fractions of traffic that went completely through other backbones. The data for 1996 through 2000 are estimates, and the wide ranges reflect the uncertainties caused by the lack of comprehensive data.

The voice network still dominated, but was likely to be surpassed by the public Internet within a year or two. In terms of bandwidth, the Internet is already dominant. However, it is hard to obtain good figures, since, as discuss later, the bandwidth of Internet backbones jumps erratically. In terms of dollars, though, voice still provides the lion's share of total revenues.

The growth rates in Internet traffic, as measured in bytes. For many purposes, it is the other measures, namely bandwidth and revenues, that are more important. The reason look at traffic is that more regularity there, and in the long run, there will be direct relations between traffic and the other measures. In particular, based on what observed so far, expect capacity to grow somewhat faster than traffic.

Table 1

Traffic on Internet backbones in US. For each year, shows estimated traffic in terabytes during December of that year

year	*TB/month*
1990	1.0
1991	2.0
1992	4.4
1993	8.3
1994	16.3
1995	?
1996	1,500
1997	2,500 - 4,000
1998	5,000 - 8,000
1999	10,000 - 16,000
2000	20,000 - 35,000

The proposal of a new form of Moore's Law, namely that a doubling of Internet traffic each year is a natural growth rate. This hypothesis is supported by the estimates of Table 1, as well as by evidence presented in of many institutions whose data traffic has been growing at about that rate for many years. It is not a law of nature, but rather, like the Moore's Law for semiconductors, a reflection of the complicated interactions of technology, economics, and sociology. Whether this 'law' continues to hold or not will have important implications for the fiber optic transmission industry. Yet more evidence of how often popular perception and subsequent technology and investment decisions are colored by myths that are easy to disprove, but which nobody had bothered to disprove for an astonishingly long time. The historical growth rates of various communication services, and how they compare to the much higher growth rate of the Internet.

Some of the various types of growth rates that are relevant in different contexts. The evidence about Internet traffic growth rates have been able to assemble. The conventional 'Moore's Law' and the analog are proposing for data traffic. A way of thinking about data traffic growth, based on an analogy with the computer industry.

Internet growth is an unusual subject, in that it has been attracting enormous attention but very little serious study. In particular, the general consensus has been that Internet traffic is doubling every three or four months. Yet no real evidence of that astronomical rate of growth was ever presented. Internet traffic did grow at such rates in 1995 and 1996, but before and since it has been about doubling each year.

Telecommunications has been a growth industry for centuries, but growth rates have generally been modest, except for a few episodes, such as the beginnings of the electric telegraph. For example, the number of pieces of mail delivered in the US grew by a factor of over 50,000 between 1800 and 2000, but that was a growth rate of about 5.6% per year. The number of phone calls in the US grew by a factor of over 230 between 1900 and 2000, for a compound annual growth rate of 5.6%. Long distance calls grew faster, about 12% per year between 1930 and 2000, and transatlantic calls faster yet. One communications industry that has been growing very rapidly recently is wireless communication.

In many other countries, wireless communication has developed faster and plays a bigger role than it does in the U.S. Still, even in the U.S., at the end of 2000, there were close to 100 million cell phones in use, and the rate of growth was far higher than for traditional wired voice services.

The cell phone example is worth keeping in mind, since it shows that volume of traffic or even the number of users has only a slight correlation to value. In the US (unlike several other countries), there were more Internet users than cell phone subscribers at the end of 2000 (around 150 million vs. about 100 million). However, the revenues of the cell phone industry were far higher than those of the Internet. Take a rough estimate of 60 million residential Internet users, and assume they pay an average of $20 per month (both slight overestimates), the total revenues from this segment come to about $15 billion. Business customers, with dedicated connections to the Internet, pay considerably less than that. For example, the 2000 revenues from business Internet connections of WorldCom (whose UUNet unit has the largest backbone in the world, often thought to carry over 30% of the total backbone traffic) were just $2.5 billion. Even in the U.S., basic Internet transport revenues are less than half those of cell phones. Yet volumes of traffic are far higher on the Internet.

The average daily time spent by a subscriber on a cell phone in the US is about 8 minutes. If count wireless communication as taking 8 Kb/s (since compression is used), the total volume of traffic generated by cell phone users in the US at the end of 2000 was only about 1,500 TB/month, a tiny fraction of the 20,000 to 35,000 TB/month traffic on US Internet backbones. The comparison of revenues from Internet connectivity to those of the cell phone industry leads naturally to the next topic, namely a comparison with the entire phone industry. Internet revenues were under $25 billion in the U.S. in 2000.

On the other hand, the revenues of the entire telephone industry (including wireless communication and data services such as private lines leased by corporations) were around $300 billion that year. Thus in terms of revenues, the Internet is still small. Furthermore, it is so intimately tied to the phone industry that it is difficult to see what its role is. The basic technologies that are used for Internet transport were developed initially for voice telephony, but were easily adopted for data. At the transport level, voice has been carried as bits for a long time. What happened is that during the late 1990s, the long distance telecommunications infrastructure has changed. It used to be dominated by the demands of voice transport, and data was a small part of what it carried. Now, however, its development is driven by data, especially Internet. For quite a long time, the volume of data was extremely small, so that even though the growth rate was higher than for voice, this did not affect the overall growth rate of the infrastructure. That was one reason the telecommunications industry has repeatedly been surprised by the demand for bandwidth in the 1990s.

Moreover, the transition from voice to data domination was complicated by the presence of several types of data, with substantially different growth rates. Another reason that the recent upsurge in demand for bandwidth was a surprise is that there had been several previous false predictions that data traffic was about to explode. The excitement of the early 1990s about the 'telecommunications superhighway' and '500 channels to the home,' to be accomplished through technologies such as hybrid fiber-coax, certainly led to large financial losses and serious disappointments. However, there were even earlier periods of extremely rapid growth followed by sudden deceleration. For example, the number of modems in the U.S. grew between 1965 and 1970 at about 60% per year, to over 150,000 at the end of that period. Had that growth rate been maintained, about 200 billion modems in the U.S. by the end of 2000, clearly an absurd number. Instead, it appears that growth in the 1970s followed the projections made around 1970, which predicted annual increases of 25 to 30%.

It is interesting to read the speculations in about the supposedly rosy prospects for electronic cash, distance education, and other data services that were supposed to power the growth of networks. In general, predicting what communications services society will accept, and how it will use them, has been very hard. In particular, even recent history is littered with technologies that seemed extremely promising at one point, such as ISDN or SMDS (Switched Multimegabit Data Services—a high speed packet switched WAN tecnology), but never attained more than a marginal role. There are two aspects of the inability to forecast the prospects of communications technologies that are worth discussing at greater length. One goes back to the earlier discussion of wireless telephony, and how the mobility offered by cell phones appears to be more important for many people than broadband Internet access.

Sometimes, though, higher bandwidth did prevail. In the early days of telephony, there was widespread lack of appreciation of how attractive it would eventually prove to be. The telephone was used primarily for business purposes, and the telegraph appeared to be adequate for that to many. Yet it was the phone that won, even though it appeared to use bandwith very wastefully when compared to the telegraph, and even though it encouraged what was often dismissed as 'idle chatter.' The attractions of instantaneous personal interactions turned out to be crucial in leading to an almost universal penetration of the telephone in industrialized countries. In the last four decades of the 20th century, though, the telecommunications industry several times attempted to extend its success with the voice telephone by introducing videotelephony. This service appeared to offer the attraction of an even deeper level of communication than voice. Yet prospective users have not only not embraced it, but have in many cases treated it with hostility. There is a growth of videoconferencing, but even that is far slower than its proponents had forecasted. For a variety of reasons that have not been completely explained, videotelephony does not appeal to people for person-to-person communication. On the other hand, mobile narrowband voice flourishes. The other aspect of the dismal record in forecasting the prospects of communications technologies that now consider is that of the nature of traffic carried.

Data networks, which in commercial settings go back about four decades, have spent essentially all this time in the shadow of the much larger voice telephone network. It was therefore natural for networking experts to continuously think of voice traffic, and in particular of the possibility of eventually carrying it as data. Looking further out, to a stage where the progress of technology appeared to offer the possibility of data networks becoming much larger than the phone networks, it was also natural to think of enriching the communications medium through the addition of video. Later the huge volume of broadcast data offered further possibilities for traffic that could be carried on data networks. The key point is what was seen as eventually filling data network was streaming multimedia traffic.

The Internet's rise to dominance was a surprise for many reasons, but one of the main ones was that it did not fit this model. Although much current work on Internet technologies is devoted to streaming multimedia, there are good reasons, why such traffic is not likely to dominate. Although it has proven hard to forecast which technologies will be widely adopted, once a service had been successfully introduced, it often showed regular growth rates for extended periods of time. The approximately 30% annual growth rate that had been projected in 1970 for data transmission appears to have held not just in the 1970s, but in the 1980s and most of the 1990s as well. There are no comprehensive statistics. However, there are a few pieces of evidence supporting those growth rates around 1980 in.

Those same growth rates appeared to also hold for long distance private line transmission in the mid 1990s, and for local data bandwidth in the late 1980s and most of the 1990s. The comprehensive data summarized in is especially interesting. During that period, installed computer power came close to doubling each year, and the new 'Information Economy' was taking root, but this was not reflected in the volume of data traffic. This low rate of growth in data transmission may have come from the high cost and poor quality of data transmission, of from other causes, such as lack of uniform standards that would enable easy data communication between companies. It may also have been caused to a large extent by the slow rate at which computation and communication technologies were adopted. Whatever the reasons, this low growth rate of approximately 30% a year in data transmission was higher than that of voice networks. Hence by the mid-1990s, the bandwidth of long distance data networks was already comparable to that of the voice network. The Internet has historically had a growth rate of close to 100% per year in the traffic it carried. It was growing with striking regularity in the early 1990s at this rate. Then it experienced a period of astronomical growth in 1995 and 1996, and then reverted to an approximate doubling each year in 1997, and has continued growing at about that rate through the end of 2000. The big question is how fast it will grow in the future. While the overwhelming preponderance of opinion all through the end of 2000 was that Internet traffic was doubling every three or four months, by early 2001 the consensus started changing. Some analysts even began projecting declines in the growth rates to the 50% per year range by around 2005. And indeed, some sources of growth did dry up. With the crash of telecom stocks, investments slowed, and many dot-coms that had been busily filling transmission pipes with their content disappeared. In a related development, corporate managements started asking for detailed justifications for new data networking expenditures, instead of rushing to endorse any proposals that came along.

At various enterprises, the growth rates of data traffic, which had been close to doubling every year in the late 1990s, began to slow down towards doubling every 18 or 24 months. It is not inconceivable that overall data traffic growth may be moving back to its historical rate of around 30% per year. At this point just remark that the dominant role of the Internet in communications, whether in terms of bandwidth of networks, or popular consciousness, is a fairly recent phenomenon. There had been extensive discussions of the 'Information Superhighway' and the 'National Information Infrastr-ucture' for a long time. Leading thinkers foresaw the possibilities for much improved communication offered by new technologies, and there was tremendous effort devoted to various systems. However, the general expectation was that the 'Information Superhighway' would be composed of a very heterogeneous collection of networks. This was true even as late as the beginnings of the Clinton presidency, in 1993 and 1994. It was only in the mid to late 1990s that the Internet was perceived as evolving towards the all-encompassing network, carrying all types of traffic.

The past 5-10 years have witnessed not only an explosion of activity, but the creation of entirely new sectors within the optical industry. As the concept of WDM began to emerge, many new companies developing WDM transport equipment came into existence. The newer enterprises pushed the older established equipment vendors to more aggressive deployment schedules and a constant downward trend for the corresponding prices of WDM transport equipment followed. In what appeared to be an almost insatiable demand for more bandwidth, a situation arose that allowed the creation of the new companies and the accompanying innovation.

Not only did new equipment vendors emerge, but also new national scale carriers were created. This trend is continuing as the concept of optical layering/networking is gaining acceptance and new optical equipment companies are being formed on a regular basis. They deal not only with 'traditional' WDM transport equipment, but also with terrestrial ultra long haul systems, regional and metro optimized systems, and various incarnations of optical cross connects. There were hundreds of developments and contributions enabling this burst of activity.

When one now speaks of the Internet, it is usually described as an evolution from ARPANET to NSFNET, and finally to the commercial Internet that now exists. Arguably, the phenomenal growth of the Internet started in 1986 with NSFNet. However, the path was very complicated and full of many twists and turns in its roughly 40 year history. From the very early research in packet switching, academia, industry, and the US government have been intertwined as partners. Ironically, the beginnings of the Internet can trace itself back to the Cold War and specifically to the launch of Sputnik in 1957. The US government formed the Advanced Research Agency (ARPA—the name was later changed to DARPA, Defense Advanced Research programme Agency, and later back to ARPA) the year after the launch with the stated goal of establishing a US lead in technology and science. As ARPA was establishing itself, there were several pivotal works in the early 1960s on packet switching and computer communications. These works and the efforts they spawned laid many of the foundations that enabled the deployment of distributed packet networks. Generically speaking, this idea is not much different from what today's Internet has become. Concurrently the National Physical Laboratory (NPL) in England deployed an experimental network called the NPL Network making use of packet switching. It utilized 768 kb/s lines. A year before the Moon landing, in 1968, the first ARPANET requests for proposals were sent out, and the first ARPANET contracts were awarded. Two of the earliest contracts went to UCLA to develop the Network Measurement Center, and to Bolt, Beranek and Newman (BBN) for the Packet Switch contract (to construct the Interface Message Processors or IMPs—effectively the routers).

One of the next major innovations for the fledgling Internet (i.e., ARPANET) was the introduction of the first host-to-host protocol called Network Control Protocal or NCP, which was first used in ARPANET in 1970. By 1972 all of the ARPANET sites had finished implementing NCP. Hence the users of ARPANET could finally begin to focus on the development of applications—another paramount driver for the phenomenal growth and sustained growth of the internet. It was also in 1970 that the first cross-country link was established for ARPANET by AT&T between UCLA and BBN. By 1971, the ARPANET had grown to 15 nodes and had 23 hosts. However, perhaps the most influential work that year was the creation of an email programme that could send messages across a distributed network.

Although there was already considerable work being done on packet networks outside the US, the first international connections to the ARPANET took place in 1973. To put the time frame in perspective this was the same year that Robert Metcalfe did his PhD which described his idea for Ethernet. Also during this year the number of ARPANET 'users' was estimated to be 2000 and that 75% of all the ARPANET traffic (in terms of bytes) was email. One needs to note that in only 1-2 years from its introduction onto the Internet email became the predominant type traffic. The same behaviour took place several years later for HTML, and to a somewhat lesser degree, this was seen for Napster—like traffic within many networks a few years later.

Several other key developments began to take place in the mid 1970s. The initial design specification for TCP published by Vint Cerf and Bob Kahn in 1974. The NCP protocol which was being utilized at the time, tended to act like a device driver, whereas the future TCP (later

TCP/IP) would be much more like a communications protocol. The evolution from ARPANET's NCP protocol to TCP (which in 1978 was split into TCP and IP) was critical in allowing the future growth and scalability of today's Internet. DARPA had three contracts to implement TCP/IP (at the time still called TCP), at Stanford (led by Cerf), BBN (led by Ray Tomlinson) and UCLA (led by Kirsten). Stan-ford produced the detailed specification and within a year there were 3 independent implementations of TCP that could interoperate. It is say that the basic reasons that led to the separation of TCP (which guaranteed reliable delivery) from IP actually came out of work that was done trying to encode and transport voice through a packet switch. It was found that a tremendous amount of buffering was needed, in order to allow for the appropriate reassembly after transmission was completed. This in turn led to trying to find a way to deliver the packets without requiring a guaranteed level of reliability.

In essence, the UDP was created to allow users to make use of IP. In addition, it was also in 1978 that the first commercial version of ARPANET came into existence as BBN opened Telenet. In 1981-82 the first plans were being made to 'migrate' from NCP to TCP. It is claimed by some that it was this event (TCP was established as THE protocol suite for ARPANET) was truly the birth of the Internet—defined as a connected set of networks, specifically those with TCP/IP. A few years later another major development occurred, which later enabled the Internet to scale with the 'explosive' growth and popularity of the future Internet. This was the development of the name server. The name server was developed at the University of Wisconsin. This made it easy for people to use the network since hosts were assigned names and it was not necessary to remember numeric addresses. Much of the credit for the invention of the DNS (domain name server) is credited to Paul Mockapetris of USC/ISI. The year 1983 was also the date for two other key developments on ARPANET.

The first one was the cutover from NCP to TCP on the ARPANET. Secondly, ARPANET was split into ARPANET and MILNET. Although the road was convoluted, this split was one of the key bifurcations points that later allowed NSFNET to come into existence. Soon thereafter the number of hosts on the ARPANET had grown to 1000, and in 1985 the first registered domain was assigned in March. In 1985 NSFNET was created with a backbone speed of 56 kb/s. Initially there were 5 supercomputing centers that were interconnected. One of the paramount benefits of this was that it allowed an explosion of connections to take place. Two years later in 1987, NSF agreed to work with MERIT Network to manage the NSFNet backbone. In 1987 the number of hosts on the Internet broke the 10,000 number. Two year later in 1989 this had grown to around 100,000, and 3 years after that in 1992 it reached the 1,000,000 value. It is noted that if look at how the number of hosts had been growing from 1984 to 1992 that it was still pretty much tracking a growth curve that was less than tripling each year.

In the 1985-86 time frame key decision was made that had very long term impact: that TCP/IP would be mandatory for the NSFNet programme. In the 1988-1990 time frame a conscious decision was made to connect the Internet to electronic mail carriers, and by 1992 most of the commercial email carriers in the US were 'like the Internet'. This was still another development that cemented email as the single most important application to take advantage of the Internet. In 1990 the ARPANET ceased to exist, and arguably NSFNet was the essence of the Internet. Commercial Internet Service Providers began to emerge (PSI, ANS, Sprint Link, to name a few) and the Commercial Internet Xchange (CIX) was organized in 1991 by commercial ISPs to provided transfer points for traffic. NSF's lifting the restriction on the commercial use of the Net was again one of the pivotal decisions. This was again a key bifurcation point, in that this helped set the stage for the complete commercialization of the Net that would follow only a few years later.

In 1991 the upgrading of the NSFNet backbone continued as the work to upgrade to a T3 (i.e., 45 Mb/s links) began. It also interesting to note that it was the next year than the term 'surfing the Internet' was first coined by Jean Armour Polly, only two years before the ARPAnet/Internet celebrated its 25th anniversary. It was in the 1993-1995 time period that several major events seemed to emerge which fueled an almost explosive growth in the popularity of the Internet. One of the key ones was the introduction of 'browsers' most notable Mosaic. This led to the creation of Netscape that went public in 1995. Even as early as 1994 WWW (i.e., predominantly html) traffic was increasing in volume on the Net. By then it was the second most popular type of traffic, surpassed only by ftp traffic. However, in 1995 WWW traffic surpassed ftp as the greatest amount of traffic. In addition the traditional online dial up systems such as AOL, Prodigy and Compuserve began to provide Internet access. In 1996 the net truly became public with the NSFNet being phased out. Soon thereafter major infrastructure improvements were made within the transport part of the Internet.

The Internet is very hard to describe. By comparison, even the voice phone system, which is a huge enterprise, far larger in terms of revenues than the Internet, is much simpler. In the phone system, the basic service is well defined and simple to describe. The users have only limited ability to interact with the system. The Internet is completely different. Users interact with the system in a multiplicity of ways, on wildy different time scales, and there are many complicated feedback loops. The problems that arise in attempting to simulate the Internet. The problems of measuring the Internet are also formidable.

There are many different measures that are relevant. For the optical fiber telecommunications industry, it is capacity that is most relevant. Unfortunately there are numerous problems in measuring capacity. Much of the fiber is not lit, and even when it is lit, often only a few wavelengths are lit. Finally, much of potential capacity is used for restoration, through SONET or other methods. In addition, even at the levels of links used for providing IP traffic, it is hard to obtain accurate capacity measurements, since few carriers provide detailed data. Further, this type of capacity has a tendency to jump suddenly, as bandwidth is usually increased in large steps such as going from OC3 to OC12, and then OC48, a phenomenon that contributes to the low utilization of data links. Thus there is little regularity in capacity growth figures. On the other hand, do find astonoshing regularity in traffic growth, which leads us to propose that a form of 'Moore's Law' applies. In the long run, expect that capacity will grow slightly faster than traffic. For many purposes other measures are important, such as the number of users, how they spend their time, how many and what types of commercial transactions they engage in, and so on.

Whether Internet traffic doubles every three months or just once a year has huge consequences for network design as well as the telecommunications equipment industry. Much of the excitement about and funding for novel technologies appear to be based on expectations of unrealistically high growth rates. The comparison of the international bandwidth for Australia and China is instructive. In December 2000, Telstra had about 1,000 Mb/s to the rest of the world, about a third of Chinese bandwidth. Thus, making allowances for other Australian carriers, can speculate that Australia may be exchanging half as much traffic with international destinations as China does, even though the latter has over 60 times the population.

The data for the first two sources (ISPs and exchange points) is not nearly as complete nor reliable as only a few years ago. However, much better data is available for the 'stable sources', and several are examined in much more detail later. Traffic that averages 100 Mb/s is equivalent to about 30 TB/month. Unfortunately the largest ISPs do not release reliable statistics. This situation was better even a couple of years ago. Much of the older data was used in previous studies. For example, MCI used to publish precise data about the traffic volumes on their Internet backbone. Even though they were among the first ISPs to stop providing official network maps, one could obtain good estimates of the MCI Internet backbone capacity from public presentations. These sources dried up when MCI was acquired by WorldCom, and the backbone was sold to Cable &Wireless.

The traffic growth rate for that backbone had been in the range of 100% a year before the change. Today, one can obtain some idea of the sizes (but not traffic) of various ISP networks. The average utilizations of the links in the AboveNet long-haul backbone during those four months were 18%, 16%, 29%, 12%, 11%, and 10%, respectively. If one just adds up the volumes for each link separately, one finds that between March 1999 and April 2001, the total volumes of traffic increased at an annual growth rate of about 200%. However, this figure has to be treated with caution, as actual traffic almost surely increased less than 200%. During this period, AboveNet expanded geographically, with links to Japan and Europe, so that at the end it probably carried packets over more hops than before. Since, interested in end-to-end traffic as seen by customers (which can be thought of as the ingress and/or egress traffic into and/or out of 'the network'), deflate the sum of traffic volumes seen on separate backbone links by the average number of hops that a packet makes over the backbones. Even when there is reliable data for a single carrier, such as AboveNet, some of the growth seen may be coming from gains in market share, both from gains within a geographical region, and from greater geographical reach, and not from general growth in the market.

Internet exchange points: When the NSF Internet backbone was phased out in early 1995, it was widely claimed that most of the Internet backbone traffic was going through the Network Access Points or NAPs, which tended to provide decent statistics on their traffic. Currently it is thought that only a small fraction of backbone traffic goes through the NAPs, while most goes through private peering connections. Furthermore, NAP statistics are either no longer available, or not as reliable. This is in sharp contrast to the situation in 1998. As documented elsewhere, there is very little that can be reliably concluded about current growth rates of Internet traffic by examining the statistics of the public NAPs in the US. However, the situation was slightly better examined a large number of international exchange points. These included LINX (the London Internet exchange), AMS-IX (the Amsterdam Internet exchange), the Slovak Internet exchange, HKIX (a commercial exchange created by the Chinese University of Hong Kong, BNIX (located in Belgium), the INEX (an Irish exchange), and FICX (the Finish exchange). Some of these show growth rates of only about doubling per year while others show much faster growth rates. Traffic interchange statistics are hard to interpret, unless one has data for most exchanges, which is virtually impossible to obtain.

Much of the growth one sees can come from ISPs moving from one exchange to another, moving their traffic from one exchange to another, or else coming to an exchange in preference to buying transit from another ISP. Consider the specific case of LINX. A large part of its growth is almost surely caused by more ISPs exchanging their traffic there. Between March 1999, and March 2000, the ranks of ISPs that are members of LINX have grown by about two thirds, based on the data on the LINX home page. Hence the average per-member traffic through LINX may have increased only around 120% during that year. The traffic from residential U.S. customers will probably begin to increase at a faster rate in the near future. The growth in the number of users is likely to diminish. However, broadband access, in the shape of cable modems and DSL (and to a lesser extent fixed wireless links) will stimulate usage.

The evidence so far is that users who switch to cable modem or DSL access increase their time online by 50 to 100%, and the total volume of data they download per month by factors of 5 to 10. A 5 or 10-fold growth in data traffic would correspond to a doubling of traffic every four months if everyone were to switch to such broadband access in a year. However, that is not going to happen. At the end of 1999, there were about 3 million households in the US with broadband access. The most ambitious projections for cable modem and DSL access call for about 13 million households to have such links in 2003, and between 50-60 million in the year 2007. That is approximately a doubling each year. The traffic from a typical residential broadband customer is likely to grow beyond the level see today, as more content becomes available, and especially as more content that requires high bandwidth is produced.

Still, it is hard to see average traffic per customer among those with broadband connections growing at more than 50% a year, say. Together with a doubling in the ranks of such customers, this might produce a tripling of traffic from this source. Since the ranks of customers with regular modems are unlikely to decrease much, if any, and since their traffic dominates, it appears that the most likely scenario will be for the total residential customer traffic growing no faster than 200% per year, and probably closer to 100% per year. Traffic at various stable institutions, corporate, academic, and governmental. Growth in traffic can be broken down into growth in the number of traffic sources, and growth in traffic per source. For LINX, much of the increase in traffic may be coming from an increase in member ISPs. For individual ISPs, much of the increase in traffic may also be coming from new customers. Yet in the end, that kind of growth is limited, as the market gets saturated.

Consider growth in traffic from large institutions that are already well wired, such as corporations and universities. Most corporations do not publicize information about their network traffic, and many do not even collect it. However, there are some exceptions. Internal corporate traffic appears to be growing much more slowly than the public Internet traffic. Data for retail private lines as well as for Frame Relay and ATM services show aggregate growth in bandwidth in a range of 30-40% per year. The growth is slow for retail private lines, and fast for Frame Relay and ATM. These rates are remarkably close to the growth rate observed in the late 1970s in the US, which was around 30% per year. Thus, it is the corporate traffic to the public Internet that is growing at 100% per year. It is also important to note that in the year 2000 over two thirds of the volume on the public Internet appeared to be business to business.

Thus, the acceleration on the overall growth rate of data traffic to about 100% per year from the old 30% or so a year appears to be a consequence of the advantages of the Internet, with its open standards and any-to-any connectivity.

The spread of Napster through universities is a good example of the last point. Napster and related tools, such as Gnutella and Wrapster, are just the forerunners of other programs for sharing of general information, and not just for disseminating pirated MP3 files. As explained elsewhere, there is already much more digital data on hard disks alone than shows up on today's Internet. Further, this situation is likely to continue.

The arrival of Napster led many institutions to either ban its use or else limit traffic rates to some parts of the campus (typically student dormitories). Push technologies were stifled at least partially because enterprise network administrators blocked them at their firewalls. Email often has size restrictions that block large attachments.

Teleconferencing is only slowly being experimented with on corporate intranets, and even packetized voice sees very limited (although growing) use. Similar constraints apply to most of the content seen on the Web. As long as a large fraction of potential users have limited bandwidth, such as through dial modems, managers of Web servers will have an incentive to keep individual pages moderate in size. Thus, one can see that Internet traffic is subject to a variety of constraints at different levels.

Some are applied by network managers, others by individual users, and the interaction of these constraints with the rising demands is fundamental what produces the growth rates observed. The ability to sustain the high growth rate of Internet traffic will require the creation of new applications that will generate huge traffic of volumes. At current growth rates, by 2005 there will be 8 times as much Internet as voice traffic (on the US long haul networks). If voice were packetized, in all likelihood the voice traffic would only account for about 3% of the Internet traffic. Thus, voice traffic will not fill the pipes that are likely to exit, and neither will traditional Web surfing. This will create a dilemma for service providers, network administrators, and equipment suppliers: to sustain the growth rates that the industry has come to depend on, and to accommodate the progress in technology, new technologies are needed. Such applications will appear disruptive to network operations today, and as such they often have to be controlled. However, tin the long run, they must be encouraged.

It is often said that everything changes so rapidly on the Internet that it is impossible to forecast far into the future. The next 'killer app' could disrupt any plans that one makes. Yet there have been just two 'killer apps' in the history of the Internet: email and the Web. Many other technologies that had been widely touted as the next 'killer app,' such as Push technology, have fizzled. Furthermore, only the Web can be said to have been truly disruptive. From the first release of the Mosaic visual browser around the middle of 1993, it apparently took under 18 months before Web traffic became dominant on Internet backbones. It appears overwhelmingly likely that it was the appearance of browsers that then led, in combination with other developments, to that abnormal spurt of a doubling of Internet traffic every three or four months in 1995 and 1996. The text-based transmissions of those services, which probably averaged only a few hundred bits per second per connected user, were replaced by the graphics-rich content of the Web, so transmission rates increased to a few thousand bits per second. Finally, flat rate access plans led to a tripling of the time that individual users spent online, as well as faster growth in number of users.

The Internet was able to support this explosion in use because it was utilizing the existing infrastructure of the telephone network. At that time, the Internet was tiny compared to the voice network. It is likely that the data network that handles control and billing for the AT&T long distance voice services by itself was carrying more traffic than the NSF Internet backbone did at its peak at the end of 1994. Today, by contrast, the public Internet is rapidly moving towards being the main network, so quantum jumps in traffic cannot be tolerated so easily. In late 1999, a new application, Napster appeared that attracted extensive attention and led to many predictions that network traffic would see a major impact. However, upon close examination this does not appear to be completely accurate, and the use of Napster has not increased growth rates much beyond the annual doubling or tripling rates, even within university environments, where Napster is most popular. That is not to say that is has not resulted in huge amounts of traffic, nor that it has not had serious impact on several major networks.

Napster provides software that enables users connected to the Internet to exchange and/or download MP3 music files. The Napster (web) site matches users seeking certain music files with other users who have those files on their computer. The Napster system preferentially uses as sources of files machines that have high bandwidth connections. This means that universities are the primary sources, since other organizations with fast dedicated links, mainly corporations, do not allow such traffic. The result is that although college students are often cited as the greatest users of MP3 files, it is the traffic from universities that gets boosted the most. Regular modem users are usually not affected, since their connections are too slow. However, the proliferation of cable modems and DSL connections that have 'always-on' high bandwidth connectivity is leading to problems for some residential users, especially since the uplink is the one that invariably has the more limited bandwidth. A key reason that Napster is of great interest to us is that similar types of sharing applications effectively turn consumers of information into providers of information. These applications will effectively turn the traditional consumer PCs into Internet servers which will output large amounts of traffic to other users.

In Napster's case this has been predominantly MP3 music files, but other programs, such as Gnutella, work with more general data. It is highly probable that such applications could be one of the key applications that fuel the continued annual doubling or tripling of data traffic.

Napster first became noticeable in the summer of 1999. Its share of the total Internet traffic on many of the university networks has grown from essentially nothing to around 25% of the total traffic by mid to late 2000. In the traffic generated by Napster and its impact on various networks was examined. The amount of Napster traffic that is by several university networks range from around 20% at some to as high as 50%. However, the numbers are often very preliminary, and in some cases they compare Napster traffic to total traffic, while in others it appears that the high values may represent a comparison only to the out traffic. In any event this is a phenomenal growth rate for any single application.

Since it started from zero and data only goes out to about a year from that time, it is risky to extrapolate this initial explosion out indefinitely. In most cases Napster has had a noticeable effect on the growth rate of traffic on this campus, but not an outlandish one. Several networks, such as that of the University of Wisconsin-Madison that Napster traffic making up as much as 30% of the total are not doing anything to limit Napster since they claim that they still have plenty of bandwidth. Others have imposed limits on the total bandwidth available to the dormitories.

The approximate doubling of transmission capacity of each fiber that as described in is analogous to the famous 'Moore's Law' in the semiconductor industry. In 1965, Gordon E. Moore, then in charge of R&D at Fairchild Semiconductor, made a simple extrapolation from three data points in his company's product history. He predicted that the number of transistors per chip would about double each year for the next 10 years. This prediction was fulfilled, but when Moore revisited the subject in 1975, he modified his projection for further progress by predicting that the doubling period would be closer to 18 months. Remarkably enough, this growth rate has been sustained over the following 25 years. There have been many predictions that progress was about to come to a screeching halt , but the most that can be said is that there may have been some slight slowdown recently, the number of transistors in leading-edge microprocessors doubles every 2.2 years.

Experts in the semiconductor area are confident that Moore's 1975 prediction for rate of improvement can be fulfilled for at least most of the next decade. Predictions similar to Moore's had been made before in other areas, and in they were made for the entire spectrum of computing and communications. However, it is Moore's Law that has entered the vernacular as a description of the steady and predictable progress of technology that improves at an exponential rate. Moore's Law results from a complex interaction of technology, sociology, and economics. No new laws of nature had to be discovered, and there have been no dramatic breakthroughs.

On the other hand, an enormous amount of research had to be carried out to overcome the numerous obstacles that were encountered. It may have been incremental research, but it required increasing ranks of very clever people to undertake it. Further, huge investments in manufacturing capacity had to be made to produce the hardware. Perhaps even more important, the resulting products had to be integrated into work and life styles of the institutions and individuals using them. For further discussions of the genesis, operations, and prospects of Moore's Law. The key point is that Moore's Law is not a natural law, but depends on a variety of factors. Still, it has held with remarkable regularity over many decades. While Moore's Law does apply to a wide variety of technologies, the actual rates of progress vary tremendously among different areas. For example, battery storage is progressing at a snail's pace, compared to microprocessor improvements. This has significant implications for mobile Internet access, limiting processor power and display quality. Display advances are more rapid than those in power storage, but nowhere near fast enough to replace paper as the preferred technology for general reading, at least not at any time in the next decade. DRAMs are growing in size in accordance with Moore's Law, but their speeds are improving slowly.

Microprocessors are rapidly increasing their speed and size, but memory buses are improving slowly. For some quantitative figures on recent progress. From the standpoint of a decade ago, had tidal waves of just about everything: processing power, main memory, disk storage, and so on. For a typical user, the details of the PC on the desktop do not matter too much. It is generally assumed that in a couple of years a new and much more powerful machine will be required to run the new applications, and that it will be bought for about the same price as the current one. In the meantime, the average utilization of the processor is low, compression is not used, and wasteful encodings of information are used.

The stress is not on optimizing the utilization of the PC's resources, but on making life easy for the user. To make life easy for the end user, though, clever engineering is employed. Because the tidal waves of different technologies are advancing at different rates, optimizing user experience requires careful architectural decisions. In particular, since processing power and storage capacity are growing the fastest, while communication within a PC is improving much more slowly, elaborate memory hierarchies are built. They start with magnetic hard disks, and proceed through several levels of caches, invisibly to the user. The resulting architecture has several interesting implications, explored in. For example, mirroring disks is becoming preferable to RAID fault tolerant schemes that are far more efficient but slower.

The density of magnetic disk storage increased at about 30% per year from 1956 to 1991, doubling every two and a half years. In the 1990s, the growth rate accelerated, and in the late 1990s increased yet again. By some accounts, the densities in disk drives are about doubling each year. For purposes, the most relevant figure will be total storage of disk drives. However, that study was prepared in 1998, and since then IDC has revised upwards its estimates for disk storage systems towards a continuation of the doubling trend. It seems safest to assume that total magnetic disk storage capacity will be doubling each year for the next decade. However, even if there is a slowdown, say to a 70% annual growth rate, this will not affect arguments too much. The key point is that storage capacity is likely to grow at rates not much slower than those of network capacity. Furthermore, total installed storage is already immense.

An interesting estimate of the volume of information in the world is presented in. It shows that already in the year 1997 on the threshold of being able to store all data that has ever been generated in digital format on hard disks. By now well past that threshold, so future growth in disk capacities will have be devoted to other types of data that we have not dealt with before. Some of that capacity will surely be devoted to duplicate storage. Most of the storage, though, will have to be filled by new types of data. The same process that is yielding faster processors and larger memories is also leading to improved cameras and sensors. These will yield huge amounts of new data, that had not been available before. It appears impossible to predict precisely what type of data this will be. Much is likely to be video storage, from cameras set up as security measures, or else ones that record every movement. There could also be huge amounts of data from medical sensors on bodies. What is clear, though, is that 'the typical piece of information will never be looked at by a human being'. There will simply not be enough of the traditional 'content', nor even of the less formal type of 'content' that individuals will be generating on their own. Huge amounts of data that is machine generated for machine use suggests that data networks will also be dominated by transfers of such data.

There will surely be an increase in the raw volume of streaming real-time traffic, as applications such as videoconferencing move onto the Internet. However, as a fraction of total traffic, such transmissions will not only decrease eventually, but may not grow much at all even in the intermediate future. The huge imbalance in volume of storage and capacities of long distance data networks means that even the majority of traditional 'content' will be transmitted as files, and not in streaming form. For more detailed arguments supporting this prediction. This development is already making its appearance with MP3, Napster, and related programs. The huge hard disk storage volumes also mean that most data will have to be generated locally. There will surely also be much duplication (such as operating systems, movies, and so on that would be stored on millions of computers). Aside from that, there will surely be huge volumes of locally generated data (such as from security cameras and medical sensors) that will be used (if at all) only in highly digested form.

A 'Moore's Law' for data traffic is different from those in other areas, since it depends in a much more direct way on user behavior. In semiconductors, consumer willingness to pay drives the research, development, and investment decisions of the industry, but the effects are indirect. In data traffic, though, changes can potentially be much faster. A residential customer with dial modem access to the Internet could increase the volume of data transfer by a factor of about five very quickly. All it would take would be installation of one of the software packages that prefetch Web sites that are of potential interest, and which fill in the slack between transmissions initiated by the user. Similarly, a university's T3 connection to the Internet could potentially be filled by a single workstation sending data to another institution. Thus any 'Moore's Law' for data traffic is by nature much more fragile than the standard 'Moore's Law' for semiconductors, for example. Thus it is remarkable that so much regularity in growth rates of data transfers.

Links to the public Internet are usually the most expensive parts of a network, and are regarded as key choke points. They are where congestion is seen most frequently at institutional networks. Yet the mere annual doubling of data traffic even at institutions that have plenty of spare capacity on their Internet links means that there are other barriers that matter. The obvious one is the public Internet itself. It is often (some would say usually) congested. A terabit pipe does not help if it is hooked up to a megabit link, and so providing a lightly utilized link to the Internet does not guarantee good end-to-end performance. Yet that is not the entire explanation either, since corporate Intranets, which tend to have adequate bandwidth, and seldom run into congestion, tend to grow no faster than a doubling of traffic each year.

There are other obstructions, such as servers, middleware, and, perhaps most important, services and user interfaces. People do not care about getting many bits. What they care about is the applications. However, applications take time to be developed, deployed, and adopted. Internet time,' where everything changes in 18 months, has a grain of truth, but is largely a myth. Except for the ascendancy of browsers, most substantial changes take 5 to 10 years. As an example, it is at least four years since voice over IP was first acclaimed as the "next big thing." Yet its impact so far has been surprisingly modest. It is coming, but it is not here today, and it won't be here tomorrow.

What is perhaps most remarkable is that even at institutions with congested links to the Internet, traffic doubles or almost doubles each year. Users appear to find the Internet attractive enough that they exert pressure on their administration to increase the capacity of the connection.

Existing constraints, such as those on email attachments, or on packetized voice, or video, as well as the basic constraint of limited bandwidth, are gradually loosened. Note that this is similar to the process that produces the standard Moore's Law for PCs. Intel, Micron, Toshiba, and the rest of the computer industry would surely produce faster advances if users bought new PCs every year. Instead, a typical PC is used for three to four years. On one hand there is pressure to keep expenditures on new equipment and software under control, and also to minimize the complexity of the computing and communications support job. On the other hand, there is pressure to upgrade, either to better support existing applications, or to introduce new ones.

Over the last three decades, the conflict between these two pressures has produced a steady progress in computers. Similar pressures appear to be in operation in data networking. In conclusion, cannot be certain that Internet traffic will continue doubling each year. The historically it has tended to double each year. Still, trends in both transmission and in other information technologies appear to provide both the demand and the supply that will allow a continuing doubling each year. Since betting against such 'Moore's laws' in other areas has been a loser's game for the last few decades, it appears safest to assume that data traffic will indeed follow the same pattern, and grow at close to 100% per year.

Much of the almost hyperactivity within the optical fiber telecommunications industry over the past few years can be traced to the perceived and real growth of the traffic on the Internet. The overall growth rate of the Internet for most of its existence was remarkably close to "doubling every year", and anticipate that this rate will continue into the foreseeable future. In effect see a type of Moore's law associated with the growth of data traffic. This type of growth rate is in sharp contrast to the historical growth rates of various methods of communications that tended to be no greater than about 10% per year. Still, even though a doubling each year represents very fast growth, it is only comparable to the rate of progress in transmission capacity. Hence we are unlikely to see the huge increases in spending on optical communication that many business plans had been based on.

Throughout the history of the Internet there have only been two 'killer applications': email and the Web. Several events conspired which allowed an unprecedented explosion in Internet traffic in the 1995-1996 time frame, and the Internet was able to handle this since it made use of the existing telephone industry infrastructure. Since the Internet is quickly approaching the point at which it is the predominant network it is very unlikely that such huge growth rates could be so easily supported in the future. It also appears that, aside from short-range perturbations, there will be neither a 'bandwidth glut' nor a 'bandwidth shortage' going into the foreseeable future, in that supply and demand will be growing at comparable rates.

IP Addressing

Today, the Internet has entered the public consciousness as the world's largest public data network, doubling in size every nine months. This is reflected in the tremendous popularity of the World Wide Web (WWW), the opportunities that businesses see in reaching customers from virtual storefronts, and the emergence of new types and methods of doing business. It is clear that expanding business and social awareness will continue to increase public demand for access to resources on the Internet. There is a direct relationship between the value of the Internet and the number of sites connected to the Internet. As the Internet grows, the value of each site's connection to the Internet increases because it provides the organization with access to an ever expanding user/

customer population. Over the past few years, the Internet has experienced two major scaling issues as it has struggled to provide continuous and uninterrupted growth:

— The eventual exhaustion of the IPv4 address space

— The ability to route traffic between the ever increasing number of networks that comprise the Internet.

The first problem is concerned with the eventual depletion of the IP address space. The current version of IP, IP version 4 (IPv4), defines a 32-bit address which means that there are only 2^{32} (4,294,967,296) IPv4 addresses available. This might seem like a large number of addresses, but as new markets open and a significant portion of the world's population becomes candidates for IP addresses, the finite number of IP addresses will eventually be exhausted. The address shortage problem is aggravated by the fact that portions of the IP address space have not been efficiently allocated. Also, the traditional model of classful addressing does not allow the address space to be used to its maximum potential.

The Address Lifetime Expectancy (ALE) Working Group of the IETF has expressed concerns that if the current address allocation policies are not modified, the Internet will experience a near to medium term exhaustion of its unallocated address pool. If the Internet's address supply problem is not solved, new users may be unable to connect to the global Internet! The second problem is caused by the rapid growth in the size of the Internet routing tables.

Internet backbone routers are required to maintain complete routing information for the Internet. Over recent years, routing tables have experienced exponential growth as increasing numbers of organizations connect to the Internet—in December 1990 there were 2,190 routes, in December 1992 there were 8,500 routes, and in December 1995 there were 30,000+ routes. Unfortunately, the routing problem cannot be solved by simply installing more router memory and increasing the size of the routing tables.

Other factors related to the capacity problem include the growing demand for CPU horsepower to compute routing table/topology changes, the increasingly dynamic nature of WWW connections and their effect on router forwarding caches, and the sheer volume of information that needs to be managed by people and machines. If the number of entries in the global routing table is allowed to increase without bounds, core routers will be forced to drop routes and portions of the Internet will become unreachable! The long term solution to these problems can be found in the widespread deployment of IP Next Generation (IPng or IPv6) towards the turn of the century. However, while the Internet community waits for IPng, IPv4 will need to be patched and modified so that the Internet can continue to provide the universal connectivity have come to expect. This patching process may cause a tremendous amount of pain and may alter some of fundamental concepts about the Internet.

When IP was first standardized in September 1981, the specification required that each system attached to an IP-based internet be assigned a unique, 32-bit Internet address value. Some systems, such as routers which have interfaces to more than one network, must be assigned a unique IP address for each network interface. The first part of an Internet address identifies the network on which the host resides, while the second part identifies the particular host on the given network.

In recent years, the network-number field has been referred to as the 'network-prefix' because the leading portion of each IP address identifies the network number. All hosts on a given network share the same network-prefix but must have a unique host-number. Similarly, any two hosts on different networks must have different network-prefixes but may have the same host-number.

Primary Address Classes

In order to provide the flexibility required to support different size networks, the designers decided that the IP address space should be divided into three different address classes—Class A, Class B, and Class C. This is often referred to as 'classful' addressing because the address space is split into three predefined classes, groupings, or categories. Each class fixes the boundary between the network-prefix and the host-number at a different point within the 32-bit address.

One of the fundamental features of classful IP addressing is that each address contains a self-encoding key that identifies the dividing point between the network-prefix and the host-number. For example, if the first two bits of an IP address are 1-0, the dividing point falls between the 15th and 16th bits. This simplified the routing system during the early years of the Internet because the original routing protocols did not supply a 'deciphering key' or 'mask' with each route to identify the length of the network-prefix.

Class A Networks (/8 Prefixes): Each Class A network address has an 8-bit network-prefix with the highest order bit set to 0 and a seven-bit network number, followed by a 24-bit host-number.

Today, it is no longer considered 'modern' to refer to a Class A network. Class A networks are now referred to as '/8s' (pronounced 'slash eight' or just 'eights') since they have an 8-bit network-prefix. A maximum of 126 (2^7-2) /8 networks can be defined. The calculation requires that the 2 is subtracted because the /8 network 0.0.0.0 is reserved for use as the default route and the /8 network 127.0.0.0 (also written 127/8 or 127.0.0.0/8) has been reserved for the 'loopback' function. Each /8 supports a maximum of 16,777,214 (2^{24}-2) hosts per network. The host calculation requires that 2 is subtracted because the all-0s ('this network') and all-1s ('broadcast') host-numbers may not be assigned to individual hosts. Since the /8 address block contains 2^{31} (2,147,483,648) individual addresses and the IPv4 address space contains a maximum of 2^{32} (4, 294, 967, 296) addresses, the /8 address space is 50% of the total IPv4 unicast address space.

Class B Networks (/16 Prefixes): Each Class B network address has a 16-bit network-prefix with the two highest order bits set to 1-0 and a 14-bit network number, followed by a 16-bit host-number. Class B networks are now referred to as"/16s" since they have a 16-bit network-prefix. A maximum of 16,384 (2^{14}) /16 networks can be defined with up to 65,534 (2^{16} -2) hosts per network. Since the entire /16 address block contains 2^{30} (1,073,741,824) addresses, it represents 25% of the total IPv4 unicast address space.

Class C Networks (/24 Prefixes): Each Class C network address has a 24-bit network-prefix with the three highest order bits set to 1-1-0 and a 21-bit network number, followed by an 8-bit host-number. Class C networks are now referred to as "/24s" since they have a 24-bit network-prefix. A maximum of 2,097,152 (2^{21}) /24 networks can be defined with up to 254 (2^8 -2) hosts per network. Since the entire /24 address block contains 2^{29} (536,870,912) addresses, it represents 12.5% (or 1/8th) of the total IPv4 unicast address space.

In addition to the three most popular classes, there are two additional classes. Class D addresses have their leading four-bits set to 1-1-1-0 and are used to support IP Multicasting. Class E addresses have their leading four-bits set to 1-1-1-1 and are reserved for experimental use.

Dotted-decimal notation

To make Internet addresses easier for human users to read and write, IP addresses are often expressed as four decimal numbers, each separated by a dot. This format is called 'dotted-decimal notation.' Dotted-decimal notation divides the 32-bit Internet address into four 8-bit (byte) fields and specifies the value of each field independently as a decimal number with the fields separated by dots. Table 2 displays the range of dotted-decimal values that can be assigned to each of the three principle address classes. The "xxx" represents the host-number field of the address which is assigned by the local network administrator.

Table 2: Dotted-decimal ranges for each address class

Address class	*Dotted-decimal notation ranges*
A (/8 prefixes)	1.xxx.xxx.xxx through 126.xxx.xxx.xxx
B (/16 prefixes)	128.0.xxx.xxx through 191.255.xxx.xxx
C (/24 prefixes)	192.0.0.xxx through 223.255.255.xxx

The original designers never envisioned that the Internet would grow into what it has become today. Many of the problems that the Internet is facing today can be traced back to the early decisions that were made during its formative years. During the early days of the Internet, the seemingly unlimited address space allowed IP addresses to be allocated to an organization based on its request rather than its actual need. As a result, addresses were freely assigned to those who asked for them without concerns about the eventual depletion of the IP address space. The decision to standardize on a 32-bit address space meant that there were only 2^{32} (4, 294, 967, 296) IPv4 addresses available.

A decision to support a slightly larger address space would have exponentially increased the number of addresses thus eliminating the current address shortage problem. The classful A, B, and C octet boundaries were easy to understand and implement, but they did not foster the efficient allocation of a finite address space. Problems resulted from the lack of a network class that was designed to support medium-sized organizations. A /24, which supports 254 hosts, is too small while a /16, which supports 65,534 hosts, is too large.

In the past, the Internet has assigned sites with several hundred hosts a single /16 address instead of a couple of /24s addresses. Unfortunately, this has resulted in a premature depletion of the /16 network address space. The only readily available addresses for medium-size organizations are /24s which have the potentially negative impact of increasing the size of the global Internet's routing table. The subsequent history of Internet addressing is focused on a series of steps that overcome these addressing issues and have supported the growth of the global Internet.

Subnetting

In 1985, RFC 950 defined a standard procedure to support the subnetting, or division, of a single Class A, B, or C network number into smaller pieces. Subnetting was introduced to overcome some of the problems that parts of the Internet were beginning to experience with the classful two-level addressing hierarchy:

— Internet routing tables were beginning to grow.

— Local administrators had to request another network number from the Internet before a new network could be installed at their site.

Both of these problems were attacked by adding another level of hierarchy to the IP addressing structure. Instead of the classful two-level hierarchy, subnetting supports a three-level hierarchy.Subnetting attacked the expanding routing table problem by ensuring that the subnet structure of a network is never visible outside of the organization's private network. The route from the Internet to any subnet of a given IP address is the same, no matter which subnet the destination host is on. This is because all subnets of a given network number use the same network-prefix but different subnet numbers. The routers within the private organization need to differentiate between the individual subnets, but as far as the Internet routers are concerned, all of the subnets in the organization are collected into a single routing table entry. This allows the local administrator to introduce arbitrary complexity into the private network without affecting the size of the Internet's routing tables. Subnetting overcame the registered number issue by assigning each organization one (or at most a few) network number(s) from the IPv4 address space.

The organization was then free to assign a distinct subnetwork number for each of its internal networks. This allows the organization to deploy additional subnets without needing to obtain a new network number from the Internet. A site with several logical networks uses subnet addressing to cover them with a single /16 (Class B) network address. The router accepts all traffic from the Internet addressed to network 130.5.0.0, and forwards traffic to the interior subnetworks based on the third octet of the classful address. The deployment of subnetting within the private network provides several benefits:

— The size of the global Internet routing table does not grow because the site administrator does not need to obtain additional address space and the routing advertisements for all of the subnets are combined into a single routing table entry.

— The local administrator has the flexibility to deploy additional subnets without obtaining a new network number from the Internet.

— Route flapping (i.e., the rapid changing of routes) within the private network does not affect the Internet routing table since Internet routers do not know about the reachability of the individual subnets—they just know about the reachability of the parent network number.

Extended-Network-Prefix

Internet routers use only the network-prefix of the destination address to route traffic to a subnetted environment. Routers within the subnetted environment use the extended-network-prefix to route traffic between the individual subnets. The extended-network-prefix is composed of the classful network-prefix and the subnet-number. The extended-network-prefix has traditionally been identified by the subnet mask.

For example, the /16 address of 130.5.0.0 and want to use the entire third octet to represent the subnet-number, need to specify a subnet mask of 255.255.255.0. The bits in the subnet mask and the Internet address have a one-to-one correspondence. The bits of the subnet mask are set to one if the system examining the address should treat the corresponding bit in the IP address as part of the extended-network-prefix. The bits in the mask are set to 0 if the system should treat the bit as part of the host-number.

The standards describing modern routing protocols often refer to the extended-network-prefix-length rather than the subnet mask. The prefix length is equal to the number of contiguous one-bits in the traditional subnet mask. This means that specifying the network address 130.5.5.25 with a subnet mask of 255.255.255.0 can also be expressed as 130.5.5.25/24. The /<prefix-length> notation is more compact and easier to understand than writing out the mask in its traditional dotted-decimal format.

However, it is important to note that modern routing protocols still carry the subnet mask. There are no Internet standard routing protocols that have a one-byte field in their header that contains the number of bits in the extended-network prefix. Rather, each routing protocol is still required to carry the complete four-octet subnet mask.

The final step is to make sure that the organization's address allocation provides enough bits to deploy the required subnet addressing plan. For example, if the organization has a single /16, it could easily deploy 4-bits for the subnet-number and 6-bits for the host number However, if the organization has several /24s and it needs to deploy 9 subnets, it may be required to subnet each of its /24s into four subnets (using 2 bits) and then build the internet by combining the subnets of 3 different /24 network numbers. An alternative solution, would be to deploy network numbers from the private address space (RFC 1918) for internal connectivity and use a Network Address Translator (NAT) to provide external Internet access.

Defining the Subnet Mask

The first step is to determine the number of bits required to define the six subnets. Since a network address can only be subnetted along binary boundaries, subnets must be created in blocks of powers of two [2 (2^1), 4 (2^2), 8 (2^3), 16 (2^4), etc.]. Thus, it is impossible to define an IP address block such that it contains exactly six subnets. For this example, the network administrator must define a block of 8 (2^3) and have two unused subnets that can be reserved for future growth. Since $8 = 2^3$, three bits are required to enumerate the eight subnets in the block. In this example, the organization is subnetting a /24 so it will need three more bits, or a /27, as the extended-network-prefix. A 27-bit extended-network-prefix can be expressed in dotted-decimal notation as 255.255.255.224. This means that each subnetwork with a 27-bit prefix represents a contiguous block of 2^5 (32) individual IP addresses. However, since the all-0s and all-1s host addresses cannot be allocated, there are 30 (2^5 -2) assignable host addresses on each subnet.

The eight subnets will be numbered 0 through 7. The XXX_2 notation indicates the binary representation of the number. The 3-bit binary representation of the decimal values 0 through 7 are: 0 (000_2),1 (001_2),2 (010_2),3 (011_2),4 (100_2),5 (101_2),6 (110_2), and 7 (111_2). In general, to define Subnet #n, the network administrator places the binary representation of n into the bits of the subnet-number field. For example, to define Subnet #6, the network administrator simply places the binary representation of 6 (110_2) into the 3-bits of the subnet-number field.

When subnetting was first defined in RFC 950, it prohibited the use of the all-0s and the all-1s subnet. The reason for this restriction was to eliminate situations that could potentially confuse a classful router. Note that today a router can be both classless and classful at the same time—it could be running RIP-1 (a classful protocol) and BGP-4 (a classless protocol) at the same time. With respect to the all-0s subnet, a router requires that each routing table update include the route/<prefix-length> pair to differentiate between a route to the all-0s subnet and a route to the entire network. For example, when using RIP-1 which does not supply a mask or prefix-length with each route, the routing advertisements for subnet 193.1.1.0/27 and for network 193.1.1.0/24 are identical - 193.1.1.0. Without somehow knowing the prefix-length or mask, a router cannot tell the difference between a route to the all-0s subnet and the route to the entire network! Regarding the all-1s subnet, a router requires that each routing table entry include the prefix-length so that it can determine if a broadcast (directed or all-subnets) should be sent only to the all-1s subnet or to the entire network. For example, when the routing table does not contain a mask or prefix-length for each route, confusion can occur because the same broadcast address (193.1.1.255) is used for both for the entire network 193.1.1.0/24 and the all-1s subnet 193.1.1.224/27. NETBuilder software permits the forwarding of traffic to a directed broadcast address but does not forward traffic to the all-subnets broadcast address.

With the development of routing protocols that supply the mask or prefix-length with each route, the address space defined by the all-0s and all-1s subnets is once again usable despite the cautions in RFC 950. As a result, vendors have begun to accommodate user demand and permit the configuration of the all-0s and all-1s subnets on router interfaces. There are three factors that determine when these subnets can be used with NETBuilder software.

— The interior gateway protocol (IGP)

— The version number of the NETBuilder software release

— The capabilities of other routers in the organization's network.

To support the deployment of the all-0s and all-1s subnets, the IGP must either carry extended-network-prefixes or have a mechanism to map each route to its extended-network-prefix. Both OSPF and I-IS-IS carry extended-network-prefixes, so they support the deployment of the all-0s and all-1s subnets in arbitrarily complex topologies.

NETBuilder software has taken a phased approach in its support for the deployment of the all-0s and all-1s subnets. Table 3 shows the NETBuilder software version number that first implemented the various features that support the deployment of these subnets. Finally, the other routers in the organization's network need to be able to correctly interpret, learn, and forward traffic to other subnetworks with all-0s and all-1s in their subnet number field.

Table 3: NETBuilder Software Features Supporting the All-0s and All-1s Subnets

Release	*Feature supported*
6.2	Permits a router interface to be configured with all-0s in the subnet field
7.0.0.6	Permits a router interface to be configured with all-1s in the subnet field
7.1	Correctly learns and forwards to routes with all-0s in the subnet field
8.3.0.2 7.2.1	Correctly learns and forwards to routes with all 1s in the subnet field

Variable Length Subnet Masks (VLSM)

In 1987, RFC 1009 specified how a subnetted network could use more than one subnet mask. When an IP network is assigned more than one subnet mask, it is considered a network with 'variable length subnet masks' since the extended-network-prefixes have different lengths. When using RIP-1, subnet masks have to be uniform across the entire network-prefix. RIP-1 allows only a single subnet mask to be used within each network number because it does not provide subnet mask information as part of its routing table update messages. In the absence of this information, RIP-1 is forced to make very simple assumptions about the mask that should be applied to any of its learned routes. How does a RIP-1 based router know what mask to apply to a route when it learns a new route from a neighbor? If the router has a subnet of the same network number assigned to a local interface, it assumes that the learned subnetwork was defined using the same mask as the locally configured interface.

However, if the router does not have a subnet of the learned network number assigned to a local interface, the router has to assume that the network is not subnetted and applies the route's natural classful mask. Assuming that Port 1 of a router has been assigned the IP address 130.24.13.1/24 and that Port 2 has been assigned the IP address 200.14.13.2/24.

If the router learns about network 130.24.36.0 from a neighbor, it applies a /24 mask since Port 1 is configured with another subnet of the 130.24.0.0 network. However, when the router learns about network 131.25.0.0 from a neighbor, it assumes a "natural" /16 mask since it has no other masking information available.

For these reasons, RIP-1 is limited to only a single subnet mask for each network number. However, there are several advantages to be gained if more than one subnet mask can be assigned to a given IP network number:

— Multiple subnet masks permit more efficient use of an organization's assigned IP address space.

— Multiple subnet masks permit route aggregation which can significantly reduce the amount of routing information at the "backbone" level within an organization's routing domain.

VLSM supports more efficient use of an organization's assigned IP address space. One of the major problems with the earlier limitation of supporting only a single subnet mask across a given network-prefix was that once the mask was selected, it locked the organization into a fixed-number of fixed-sized subnets. For example, assume that a network administrator decided to configure the 130.5.0.0/16 network with a /22 extended-network-prefix. Since a subnetted network could have only a single mask, the network administrator was still required to assign the 20 or 30 hosts to a subnet with a 22-bit prefix.

This assignment would waste approximately 1,000 IP host addresses for each small subnet deployed! Limiting the association of a network number with a single mask did not encourage the flexible and efficient use of an organization's address space. One solution to this problem was to allow a subnetted network to be assigned more than one subnet mask. Assume that in the previous example, the network administrator is also allowed to configure the 130.5.0.0/16 network with a /26 extended-network-prefix. A /16 network address with a /26 extended-network prefix permits 1024 subnets (2^{10}), each of which supports a maximum of 62 hosts (2^6 -2). The /26 prefix would be ideal for small subnets with less than 60 hosts, while the /22 prefix is well suited for larger subnets containing up to 1000 hosts.

VLSM also allows the recursive division of an organization's address space so that it can be reassembled and aggregated to reduce the amount of routing information at the top level. Conceptually, a network is first divided into subnets, some of the subnets are further divided into sub-subnets, and some of the sub-subnets are divided into sub 2-subnets. This allows the detailed structure of routing information for one subnet group to be hidden from routers in another subnet group.

The 11.1.0.0/16 subnet is then configured with a /24 extended-network-prefix and the 11.253.0.0/16 subnet is configured with a /19 extended-network-prefix. The recursive process does not require that the same extended-network-prefix be assigned at each level of the recursion. Also, the recursive sub-division of the organization's address space can be carried out as far as the network administrator needs to take it.

When developing a VLSM design, the network designer must recursively ask the same set of questions as for a traditional subnet design. At each level, the design team must make sure that they have enough extra bits to support the required number of sub-entities in the next and further levels of recursion. Assume that a network is spread out over a number of sites. For example, if an organization has three campuses today it probably needs 3-bits of subnetting ($2^3 = 8$) to allow the addition of more campuses in the future. Now, within each campus, there is likely to be a secondary level of subnetting to identify each building. Finally, within each building, a third level of subnetting might identify each of the individual workgroups. Following this hierarchical model, the top level is determined by the number of campuses, the mid-level is based on the number of buildings at each site, and the lowest level is determined by the 'maximum number of subnets/maximum number of users per subnet' in each building.

The deployment of a hierarchical subnetting scheme requires careful planning. It is essential that the network designers recursively work their way down through their addressing plan until they get to the bottom level. At the bottom level, they must make sure that the leaf subnets are large enough to support the required number of hosts. When the addressing plan is deployed, the addresses from each site will be aggregable into a single address block that keeps the backbone routing tables from becoming too large.

The successful deployment of VLSM has three prerequisites:

— The routing protocols must carry extended-network-prefix information with each route advertisement.

— All routers must implement a consistent forwarding algorithm based on the 'longest match.'

— For route aggregation to occur, addresses must be assigned so that they have topological significance.

Since OSPF and I-IS-IS convey the extended-network-prefix information with each route, the VLSM subnets can be scattered throughout an organization's topology. However, to support hierarchical routing and reduce the size of an organization's routing tables, addresses should be assigned so that they are topologically significant. Hierarchical routing requires that addresses be assigned to reflect the actual network topology. This reduces the amount of routing information by taking the set of addresses assigned to a particular region of the topology, and aggregating them into a single routing advertisement for the entire set.

Classless Inter-Domain Routing (CIDR)

By 1992, the exponential growth of the Internet was beginning to raise serious concerns among members of the IETF about the ability of the Internet's routing system to scale and support future growth. These problems were related to:

— The near-term exhaustion of the Class B network address space

— The rapid growth in the size of the global Internet's routing tables

The eventual exhaustion of the 32-bit IPv4 address space Projected Internet growth figures made it clear that the first two problems were likely to become critical by 1994 or 1995. The response to these immediate challenges was the development of the concept of Supernetting or Classless Inter-Domain Routing (CIDR). The third problem, which is of a more long-term nature, is currently being explored by the IP Next Generation (IPng or IPv6) working group of the IETF. CIDR was officially documented in September 1993 in RFC 1517, 1518, 1519, and 1520. CIDR supports two important features that benefit the global Internet routing system:

— CIDR eliminates the traditional concept of Class A, Class B, and Class C network addresses. This enables the efficient allocation of the IPv4 address space which will allow the continued growth of the Internet until IPv6 is deployed.

— CIDR supports route aggregation where a single routing table entry can represent the address space of perhaps thousands of traditional classful routes. This allows a single routing table entry to specify how to route traffic to many individual network addresses. Route aggregation helps control the amount of routing information in the Internet's backbone routers, reduces route flapping (rapid changes in route availability), and eases the local administrative burden of updating external routing information.

CIDR eliminates the traditional concept of Class A, Class B, and Class C network addresses and replaces them with the generalized concept of a 'network-prefix.' Routers use the network-prefix, rather than the first 3 bits of the IP address, to determine the dividing point between the network number and the host number. As a result, CIDR supports the deployment of arbitrarily sized networks rather than the standard 8-bit, 16-bit, or 24-bit network numbers associated with classful addressing. In the CIDR model, each piece of routing information is advertised with a bit mask (or prefix-length). The prefix-length is a way of specifying the number of leftmost contiguous bits in the network-portion of each routing table entry. For example, a network with 20 bits of network-number and 12-bits of host-number would be advertised with a 20-bit prefix length (a /20). The clever thing is that the IP address advertised with the /20 prefix could be a former Class A, Class B, or Class C. Routers that support CIDR do not make assumptions based on the first 3-bits of the address, they rely on the prefix-length information provided with the route. In a classless environment, prefixes are viewed as bitwise contiguous blocks of the IP address space. For example, all prefixes with a /20 prefix represent the same amount of address space (2 12 or 4,096 host addresses). Furthermore, a /20 prefix can be assigned to a traditional Class A, Class B, or Class C network number.

It is important to note that there may be severe host implications when deploy CIDR based networks. Since many hosts are classful, their user interface will not permit them to be configured with a mask that is shorter than the "natural" mask for a traditional classful address. For example, potential problems could exist if wanted to deploy 200.25.16.0 as a /20 to define a network capable of supporting 4,094 (2^{12} -2) hosts. The software executing on each end station might not allow a traditional Class C (200.25.16.0) to be configured with a 20-bit mask since the natural mask for a Class C network is a 24-bit mask. If the host software supports CIDR, it will permit shorter masks to be configured. However, there will be no host problems if were to deploy the 200.25.16.0/20 (a traditional Class C) allocation as a block of 16 /24s since non-CIDR hosts will interpret their local /24 as a Class C. Likewise, 130.14.0.0/16 (a traditional Class B) could be deployed as a block of 255 /24s since the hosts will interpret the /24s as subnets of a /16. If host software supports the configuration of shorter than expected masks, the network manager has tremendous flexibility in network design and address allocation.

In a classful environment, an Internet Service Provider (ISP) can only allocate /8, /16, or /24 addresses. In a CIDR environment, the ISP can carve out a block of its registered address space that specifically meets the needs of each client, provides additional room for growth, and does not waste a scarce resource. Assume that an ISP has been assigned the address block 206.0.64.0/18. This block represents 16,384 (2^{14}) IP addresses which can be interpreted as 64 /24s. If a client requires 800 host addresses, rather than assigning a Class B (and wasting ~64,700 addresses) or four individual Class Cs (and introducing 4 new routes into the global Internet routing tables), the ISP could assign the client the address block 206.0.68.0/22, a block of 1,024 (2^{10}) IP addresses (4 contiguous /24s). However, in a classless environment, the ISP is free to cut up the pie any way it wants. It could slice up the original pie into 2 pieces (each ½ of the address space) and assign one portion to Organization A, then cut the other half into 2 pieces (each ¼ of the address space) and assign one piece to Organization B, and finally slice the remaining fourth into 2 pieces (each 1/8 of the address space) and assign it to Organization C and Organization D. Each of the individual organizations is free to allocate the address space within its "Intranetwork" as it sees fit.

If CIDR appears to have the familiar look and feel of VLSM. CIDR and VLSM are essentially the same thing since they both allow a portion of the IP address space to be recursively divided into subsequently smaller pieces. The difference is that with VLSM, the recursion is performed on the address space previously assigned to an organization and is invisible to the global Internet. CIDR, on the other hand, permits the recursive allocation of an address block by an Internet Registry to a high-level ISP, to a mid-level ISP, to a low-level ISP, and finally to a private organization's network. Just like VLSM, the successful deployment of CIDR has three prerequisites:

— The routing protocols must carry network-prefix information with each route advertisement.

— All routers must implement a consistent forwarding algorithm based on the "longest match."

— For route aggregation to occur, addresses must be assigned so that they are topologically significant.

Another important benefit of CIDR is that it plays an important role in controlling the growth of the Internet's routing tables. The reduction of routing information requires that the Internet be divided into addressing domains. Within a domain, detailed information is available about all of the networks that reside in the domain. Outside of an addressing domain, only the common network prefix is advertised.

Routing in a classless environment

The "best" thing for the size of the Internet's routing tables would be to have Organization A obtain a block of ISP #2's address space and renumber. This would allow the eight networks assigned to Organization A to be hidden behind the aggregate routing advertisement of ISP #2. Unfortunately, renumbering is a labor-intensive task which could be very difficult, if not impossible, for Organization A. The "best" thing for Organization A is to retain ownership of its address space and have ISP #2 advertise an "exception" (more specific) route into the Internet. The exception route allows all traffic for 200.25.0.0/16 to be sent to ISP #1, with the exception of the traffic to 200.25.16.0/21. This is accomplished by having ISP #2 advertise, in addition to its own 199.30.0.0/16 block, a route for 200.25.16.0/21. Using the "longest match" forwarding algorithm, Internet routers will route traffic addressed to host 200.25.17.25 to ISP #2 which will in turn route the traffic to Organization A.

NETBuilder support for CIDR

— Support for CIDR has been implemented on the NETBuilder:

— NETBuilder software implements BGP-4. Support for CIDR is a significant part of the improvements made to BGP-4.

— NETBuilder software uses a routing table structure that understands a network number advertised with a prefix that is shorter than the natural mask. The NETBuilder's routing table and forwarding process ignore the traditional IP address Class and are capable of accepting any network/mask combination that it receives.

— NETBuilder software is capable of performing aggregation by way of BGP-4 configuration parameters. Also, the OSPF AreaRange parameter allows VLSM-based aggregation to be performed within an autonomous system. The network administrator may specify exactly what network numbers and masks are advertised outside of each area or domain.

Scaling the Internet Address Space

The turn of the century, the problems of IPv4 address shortages and expanding Internet routing tables are still with us. The good news is that CIDR is working. The bad news is that recent growth trends indicate that the number of Internet routes is beginning to, once again, increase at an exponential rate. The Internet must find a way to keep the routing table growth linear. The IETF is continuing its efforts to develop solutions that will overcome these problems, enabling the continued growth and scalability of the Internet.

RFC 1917 requests that the Internet community return unused address blocks to the Internet Assigned Numbers Authority (IANA) for redistribution. This includes unused network numbers, addresses for networks that will never be connected to the global

Internet for security reasons, and sites that are using a small percentage of their address space. RFC 1917 also petitions ISPs to return unused network-prefixes that are outside of their assigned address blocks. It will be interesting to see how the Internet community responds since many organizations with unused addresses don't want to return them because they are viewed as an asset.

RFC 1918 requests that organizations make use of the private Internet address space for hosts that require IP connectivity within their enterprise network, but do not require external connections to the global Internet. For this purpose, the IANA has reserved the following three address blocks for private internets:

10.0.0.0 - 10.255.255.255	(10/8 prefix)
172.16.0.0 - 172.31.255.255	(172.16/12 prefix)
192.168.0.0 - 192.168.255.255	(192.168/16 prefix)

Any organization that elects to use addresses from these reserved blocks can do so without contacting the IANA or an Internet registry. Since these addresses are never injected into the global Internet routing system, the address space can simultaneously be used by many different organizations. The disadvantage to this addressing scheme is that it requires an organization to use a Network Address Translator (NAT) for global Internet access. However, the use of the private address space and a NAT make it much easier for clients to change their ISP without the need to renumber or 'punch holes' in a previously aggregated advertisement. The benefits of this addressing scheme to the Internet is that it reduces the demand for IP addresses so large organizations may require only a small block of the globally unique IPv4 address space.

An Internet draft, "Observations on the use of Components of the Class A Address Space within the Internet" <draft-ietf-cidrd-classa-01.txt>, explores the allocation of the upper-half of the currently reserved Class A address space through delegated registries. As the demand for IP addresses continues to grow, it appears that it may be necessary to eventually allocate the 64.0.0.0/2 address space. Note that the 64.0.0.0/2 address block is huge and represents 25% of the IPv4 unicast address space.

Implications of address allocation policies

An Internet draft , "Implications of Various Address Allocation Policies for Internet Routing" <draft-ietf-cidrd-addr-ownership-07.txt>, discusses the fundamental issues that must be considered as the Internet develops a new unicast address allocation and management policies. The draft compares the benefits and limitations of an "address ownership" policy with an "address lending" policy. 'Address ownership' means that when an address block is assigned to an organization, it remains allocated to that organization for as long as the organization wants to keep it. This means that the address block is 'portable' and that the organization would be able to use it to gain access to the Internet no matter where the organization connects to the Internet. On the other hand, 'address lending' means that an organization obtains its address block on a 'loan' basis. If the loan ends, the organization can no longer use the borrowed address block, must obtain new addresses, and renumber before using them.

Hierarchical routing requires that addresses reflect the network topology in order to permit route aggregation. The draft argues that there are two fundamental problems that break the hierarchical addressing and routing model supported by CIDR:

— The continued existence of pre-CIDR routes that cannot be aggregated.

— Organizations that switch ISPs and continue to use addresses from their previous ISP's address block. The new ISP cannot aggregate the old address block as part of its aggregation, so it must inject an exception route into the Internet. If the number of exception routes continues to increases, they will erode the benefits of CIDR and prevent the scalability of the Internet's routing system.

The draft concludes with the recommendation that large providers, which can express their destinations with a single prefix, be assigned address blocks following the 'address ownership' model. However, all allocations from these providers to a downstream clients should follow the 'address lending' model. This means that if an organization changes its provider, the loan is canceled and the client will be required to renumber. This draft has generated a tremendous amount of discussion within the Internet community about the concept of address ownership and what it means in the context of global routing. The authors present a strong argument that the Internet has to make a choice between either address ownership for all or a routable Internet—it can't have both! Smaller organizations that want to own their addresses have concerns about the difficulty of renumbering and their lack of self-determination if their provider or their provider's upstream provider changes its provider.

Procedures for Internet/Enterprise Renumbering (PIER) In the face of the 'address ownership' vs. 'address lending' debate, it is clear that renumbering may become a critical issue in the late 1990s. Procedures for Internet/ Enterprise Renumbering (PIER) is a working group of the IETF charged with the task of developing a renumbering strategy. RFC 1916 is a request by PIER for the Internet community to provide assistance in the development of a series of documents describing how an organization might proceed to renumber its network. The ultimate goal of these documents is to provide education and practical experience to the Internet community.

An Internet draft ,"Suggestions for Market-Based Allocation of IP Address Blocks" <draft-ietf-cidrd-blocks-00.txt>, is a proposal to make IPv4 address assignments transferable and condones the exchange of money as part of the transfer procedure. It suggests that the Internet community embrace the profit motive as an incentive to motivate organizations to act in ways that will improve resource use. This proposal goes hand-in-hand with another proposal to introduce financial incentives for route aggregation.

3

Marketing on Net

The term "E-commerce" has been in wide and somewhat indiscriminate use for a number of years, electronic commerce is such a broad concept that it is difficult to be dogmatic about what should be included in the scope. Many are discovering just how international the Internet really is, processing orders not only from the next town or state, but from the next continent, too. That presents new challenges to sellers who have never shipped overseas and may have little experience with the taxes, duties and customs laws involved.

The United States and 28 other countries, working together as members of the Organization for Economic Cooperation and Development, have signed on to new guidelines. The guidelines: set out principles for voluntary "codes of conduct" for businesses involved in electronic commerce; offer guidance to governments in evaluating their consumer protection laws regarding electronic commerce; and, give consumers advice about what to expect and what to look for when shopping online. The goal is to build consumer confidence in the global electronic marketplace by working to ensure that consumers are just as safe when shopping online as when shopping offline-no matter where they live or where the company they do business with is based. E-Businesses that adhere to the guidelines:

— *Use fair business, advertising and marketing practices*: They provide truthful, accurate and complete information to consumers, and avoid deceptive, misleading or unfair claims, omissions or practices. The businesses can back up all claims, such as claims about how well a product works or how quickly a product will arrive.

— *Provide accurate, clear and easily accessible information about the company and the goods or services it offers:* They disclose the information consumers need to understand whom they're dealing with and what they're buying. These businesses post the company's name, its physical address, including the country, and an email address or telephone number consumers can use if they have questions or problems. They also provide a clear, complete description of the product or service being offered.

— *Disclose full information about the terms, conditions and costs of the transaction*: They provide consumers a full, itemized list of costs involved in the transaction, designating the currency involved, as well as terms of delivery or performance, and terms, conditions and methods of payment. If applicable and appropriate to a transaction, these businesses also include information about restrictions, limitations or conditions of the purchase; instructions for proper use of the product and any safety and health care warnings; warranties and guarantees; cancellation or refund policies; and whether after-sale service is available. If it's possible to carry out a transaction in more than one language, they make available all important terms and conditions in each language.

— *Ensure that consumers know they are making a commitment to buy before closing the deal*: These businesses take steps to protect consumers who are merely "surfing" the 'Net from unknowingly entering into a sales contract. They give the consumer a chance to change the order before committing to the purchase or to cancel it altogether. They also allow consumers to keep a record of the transaction.

— *Provide an easy-to-use and secure method for online payments*: They adopt security measures appropriate to the transactions to make sure that personal information is less vulnerable to hackers.

— *Protect consumer privacy during electronic commerce transactions*: They disclose their privacy policies or information practice statements prominently on their websites, and offer people choices about how their personal information is used. They give consumers the opportunity to refuse having their personal information shared with others or used for promotional purposes.

— *Address consumer complaints and difficulties*: They have policies and procedures to address consumer problems quickly and fairly, and without excessive cost or inconvenience to the consumer. They also take advantage of alternative dispute resolution mechanisms.

— *Adopt fair, effective and easy to understand self-regulatory policies and procedures*: They extend to electronic commerce the same basic level of protections that cover other forms of commerce. The agreement encourages businesses to work with consumer representatives to develop policies and procedures that give consumers the tools they need to make informed decisions and to resolve complaints.

— *Help educate consumers about electronic commerce*: They are helping create a consumer-friendly electronic marketplace. These businesses work with governments and consumer representatives to ensure that consumers understand their rights and responsibilities when participating in online commerce.

Advanced Technology Program (ATP) provides competitive, cost-shared awards for industry to develop high-risk, enabling technologies with broad-based economic benefits. The ATP seeks to help industry fill the gap between basic research and product development, and to invest in technology that wouldn't be developed in a competitive time frame without government cost sharing.

Opportunity for the ATP to make a major difference by supporting work that is unique or complementary to other industrial and government efforts, that offers timely and significant acceleration of research progress, and that requires a critical mass of funding. Because a large number of technology ideas have been submitted to the ATP in the area of electronic commerce, specifically internet commerce, the ATP is seeking industry's input to determine whether a focused program in electronic commerce is warranted. ATP has funded projects related to electronic commerce through General Competitions and through Focused Program competitions in Inform ation Infrastructure for Healthcare, Component-Based

Software, and Technologies for the Integration of Manufacturing Applications. Each project is cost-shared between industry and government, and ATP's average contribution is approximately one million dollars per year. The ATP is a unique partnership between government and private industry to accelerate the development of high-risk technologies that promise significant commercial payoffs and widespread benefits for the economy.

Electronic Data Interchange

Using electronic channels in ordering is no new phenomenon. Electronic commerce between companies existed long before the e-business boom seen the recent half decade. At that time, prior to the Internet's breakthrough, focus was on one-to-one relations, primary in form of EDI (Electronic Data Interchange). While EDI is mainly used to send orders and invoices between pairs of companies, the Internet based e-business expands these possibilities with low-costs, global access, aggregated information, customer support capabilities, searchable product information etc. One of the major disadvantages with EDI has been the cost related to implementation and maintenance of the systems. Due to this, the EDI electronic commerce is not suitable in many-to-many or one-to-many situations. However, already implemented EDI-connections that, for example, handle automatically generated transactions based on inventory replenishment rules from an ERP-system can be very efficient and therefore profitable. When the Internet began to be widely used, some companies started to set up web sites where their customers could browse and, in some cases, buy products.

The first adopters were companies with a manageable sales channel conflict and technology-friendly customers. Still today, most companies only use the web as a marketing channel and only 15 percent of the companies having a web site are able to accept orders via their sites. Some companies have developed the idea of marketing via the Internet and have begun to form virtual hubs, often called electronic marketplaces, where buyers and sellers can meet. At these hubs, products and services from a wide range of supply units can be offered as well as a total assortment from one individual supplier. In some cases the hubs also can support the business processes before, during and after the order. Two years ago the barber said since he couldn't ship haircuts in the mail and his customers couldn't FedEx their heads, the Internet was useless for him. As a few months ago, he is ordering replacements supplies online and accepting appointments via e-mail".

Marketplaces have always played a central role when conducting business. The marketplace, electronic or not, has three major tasks: to match sellers and buyers, to facilitate transactions between the seller and the buyer and to provide an infrastructure including a legal and regulatory framework. The electronic marketplaces can facilitate these functions by offering lower search costs for the sellers and buyers to find each other and by setting standards for how purchases should be accomplished. How the electronic marketplaces will make the information transactions easier and more effective, which makes it possible for the suppliers to customize their offerings depending upon knowledge about the customer. Furthermore, for products that can be distributed electronically, e.g. software, music and texts, the electronic marketplaces can act as stores where the customers can pick their products off the shelf and have them delivered at once.

Electronic marketplace

There are various definitions of what an electronic marketplace or emarketplace really is. An e-marketplace is a site on the Internet where goods and services can be bought from a wide range of suppliers by several buyers. Net Market Makers adds in their definition that the participants should be able to conduct business "without compromising individual processes and relationships among the participants". More general and argue that it is a meeting-point where suppliers and buyers can interact online, i.e. not only on the Internet. An emarketplace can consist of one single producer selling its goods and services to its customers, which is different from the one stated above since the previous definition demands several sellers. Several authors claim that there are different ways by which the emarketplace could be managed. Different authors use the electronic marketplace notation in different ways. Consider that an emarketplace is an electronic hub on an Intranet, an Extranet or the Internet where one or more different sellers and buyers can interact.

This implicates think that an emarketplace can be used within one single business group or a supply chain as well as between different companies in different industries. However, this use of the concept is not concordant with all other authors' usage of the notation even though most authors seem to agree that the emarketplace concept is broad without clear borders. The notation where an emarketplace must include several sellers and several buyers is a subgroup to electronic hub concept. To avoid misunderstandings use electronic hub explicit mean emarketplaces which are within one single company.

Electronic hubs within a single company

A growing concept today is electronic hubs as internal trading-places on companies' Intranets, sometimes called private e-hubs or private emarketplaces. These are most common in large business groups, where different business units interact in a similar way as on the external market. The private e-hub can be used to make companies' processes more efficient, cut lead times and to support an increased information flow. The private e-hub is very similar to an external emarketplace. In both cases, participators are using the e-hub to exchange information and products. While the public emarketplace may have products from numerous different companies the private variant may have products and services from different units within the same company.

Electronic hubs

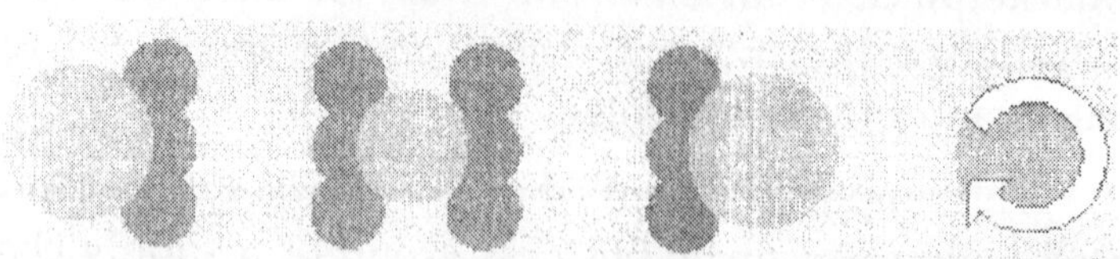

One seller, many buyers | Many sellers, many buyers | Many sellers, one buyer | Internal within a company

Figure 1: Electronic hub as a superior notation of all types ofemarketplaces

The same holds for the buyer side where the private e-hub might interconnect sales companies at different markets with the supplying part of the parent company. The main differences between emarketplaces within a single business group and those where different companies interact are:

— Level of existing business relationships. Private e-hubs consist of established networks of supply chain partners, while public emarketplaces often are more focused on new customers and partners.

— Level of information exchange. Private e-hubs tend to have a more detailed planning and information exchange than public emarketplaces.

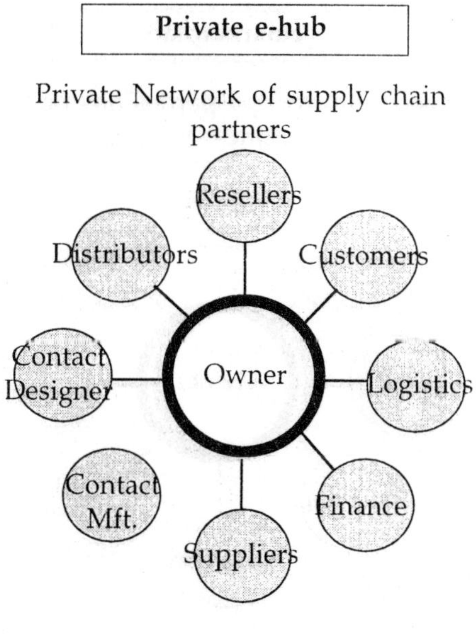

Another difference between the two concepts is the ownership. The private e-hub is governed by one of the parties within the company or the supply chain, for example a logistics department. On other hand, an external company can govern the public emarketplace. However, the purpose and functions of private and public emarketplaces are very similar. Both are meant to be a point where suppliers and sellers can meet to conduct business. They should simplify transactions and decrease the influence from distance between the interacting units. In addition to this, many of the private e-hubs as well as the public electronic marketplaces have supplementary functions as logistics, finance etc. to provide a complete offer. Therefore, believe that most of the theories, which were originally developed for public emarketplaces, can be used when discussing private e-hubs as well.

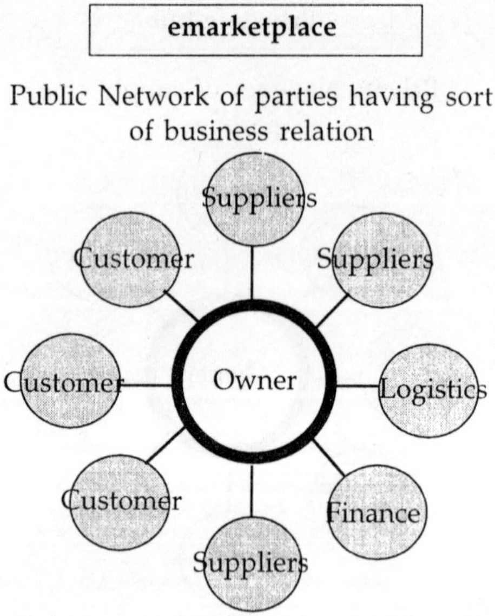

Figure 2: The private hub and the emarketplace concepts are very similar.

Categorization of emarketplaces

The emarketplaces can be categorized in several ways. In different types of emarketplaces classified by ownership, focus, pricing mechanism and how the customers buy. A natural classification of emarketplaces is by whom the marketplace is owned or controlled; this is irrespective of whether the emarketplace acts in the internal supply chain or at the public market. Many authors describe three major types of emarketplaces divided by this aspect as presented below.

emarketplaces controlled by suppliers

The first model in this categorization is the emarketplaces controlled by suppliers. According to Net Market Makers this type of emarketplaces was the first ones. They are often developed when one or more suppliers begin to use the Internet as a new sales or distribution channel, hoping that this will lead to a more efficient order or payment process. Companies using this model are often well established with a dominant market share or companies serving a fragmented market with many small customers. Kaplan & Sawhney also mention that these types of emarketplaces can serve as a forward aggregator that collects many orders from small customers so that larger orders can be sent to the sub-suppliers. An example of an often-quoted supplier-controlled emarketplace is the one handled by Cisco. That marketplace enables buyers to configure their networks, check order status and lead times, confer with technical experts, etc. At the same time as that marketplace facilitates the buying process for Cisco's customers, Cisco has managed to increase its turnover substantially with the same sales force.

Buyer-controlled marketplaces

This model is the opposite of the supplier-controlled emarketplaces. Buyer-controlled emarketplaces are set up by one or more buyers to gain advantages in form of reduced prices, smoother logistics, lower administrative costs, a more efficient procurement process, etc. The suppliers are getting requests to publish their product catalog and prices on these marketplaces. If the buyers do not have enough purchasing power, it is common that the emarketplace involves some sort of intermediary. These intermediaries act as agents or aggregators trying to find the best conditions for its owners. Sometimes this type of marketplace can be compared to reverse auctions with one or only a few buyers but a large number of sellers trying to bid under each other. Many of the buyer-controlled emarketplaces are private and inside the firewall of the buyer. However, there are also public buyer-controlled emarketplaces to which new buyers can affiliate that makes the emarketplace grow. A famous example of this type of emarketplace is Covisint. This emarketplace is set up a number of companies in the automotive industry in order to fulfill the needs of manufacturing input from their suppliers.

Neutral marketplaces

The third model in this categorization is emarketplaces independent from both suppliers and buyers. Instead a third part, a market maker, owns the marketplace and invites participators. This model can sound attractive since neither the buyer's nor the supplier's side has the control, a fact that could lead to a more efficient market. However, there are obstacles that the market maker has to overcome. One problem is the "chicken and egg" dilemma; no sellers want to participate unless a sufficient number of customers are affiliated to the emarketplace and vice versa. The fact that the sellers often join these emarketplaces at the expense of their traditional sales channel forces the market makers to prove that the pros will exceed the cons for the supplier. The market maker can earn money from the emarketplaces in numerous ways. A few examples are: transaction fees, subscription fees, advertising and data mining.

The neutral emarketplace has the best odds for success in a market that is fragmented on both the supplier's and buyer's side. At these markets the neutral marketplace can reduce transaction costs by aggregating order and supply as well as improving matching. Markets that are only fragmented on one side are more suitable for biased emarketplaces, i.e. an emarketplace controlled by a party with certain interests, for example buyers and suppliers. An example is be Band-X.com where telecom operators can sell and purchase telecommunications capacity.

Focus of the emarketplace

Depending on what goods and services sold at the emarketplace it can be categorized by its focus. There are two major groupings described by various authors: based on products and on industries.

Product-focused

The emarketplaces focused on products, sometimes called horizontal emarketplaces, serve several industries with the same products. The perhaps most well-known emarketplaces with this focus are the many emarketplaces set up to handle MRO (Maintenance, Repair and Operation), i.e. products that companies do not need in their core business but as support. However, the product-focused emarketplaces can also include services. One of these emarketplaces is Ericsson's Click-to-Buy where employees can order non-production materials such as office supplies and consultant services online. This type of focused emarketplaces can bring value to both suppliers and buyers if the market is fragmented and if the cost of conducting purchase is high compared to the value of the goods and services.

Industry-focused

The second kind of emarketplaces in this categorization is the ones focused on a particular industry, sometimes called vertical emarketplaces. These emarketplaces can for example be focused on serving the telecom industry by selling products unique for this industry. Companies get involved in these emarketplaces to buy and sell products that are strategic for their business. There are several reasons to have an emarketplace focusing on a particular type of industry. One reason is to create a critical mass of key suppliers and buyers interested in the products processed at the marketplace. Others are to disseminate knowledge within the industry and to remove inefficiencies in the existing supply chain.

The pricing mechanism used can also categorize the emarketplaces. There are four different classes of price mechanisms that emarketplaces can use:

Catalog model: This model consists of product catalogs presented on the emarketplace. The model creates value for the participants by aggregating fragmented suppliers and buyers who transact often for relatively cheap products. Most preferable, the participants should be pre-qualified and have predefined business rules.

Auction models: This model is the one if non-standard, used or non-saleable returned products should be bought or sold at a market where the perceptions of the product's value differ among the participants. Another application is when there are only a few copies of a product.

Exchange models: Marketplaces with this model work as stock exchanges. A real-time bid-ask matching process is necessary as well as marketwide price determination. To gain high liquidity it is important that the products sold are standardized without need for customization. The model suits best for markets where the prices are rather volatile.

Barter models: Barter has traditionally been used in inflationary economics with shortage of a stable currency. Today emarketplaces can be set up for bartering manufacturing or transportation capacity.

The four classes of price mechanisms they presented another way to categorize emarketplaces combining the pricing mechanism with the focus of the emarketplace. This gives an interesting framework for deciding which type of price mechanism should be used. In an article in Harvard Business Review Kaplan & Sawhney presented a classification that starts from how businesses buy and what they buy. The purchases can be classified into manufacturing and operational inputs. Manufacturing inputs consist of products that go directly into the production while operational input is not industry specific but the same products for several industries. The authors acknowledge that manufacturing inputs normally are traded on an industry-focused marketplace while operational input is more likely to traded on a product-focused marketplace.

A second distinction make is to differentiate between how the products are bought, systematic or spot sourcing. Systematic sourcing involves negotiated long-term contracts with chosen opponents and close relationships while spot sourcing is characterized by a goal to fulfill an immediate need at the lowest possible cost. These two distinctions form the B2B Matrix where emarketplaces can be placed depending on their properties.

MRO Hubs: Emarketplaces in this category are horizontal markets where products are sold with a catalog pricing mechanism. The goods tend to be low-value products with relatively high transaction costs.

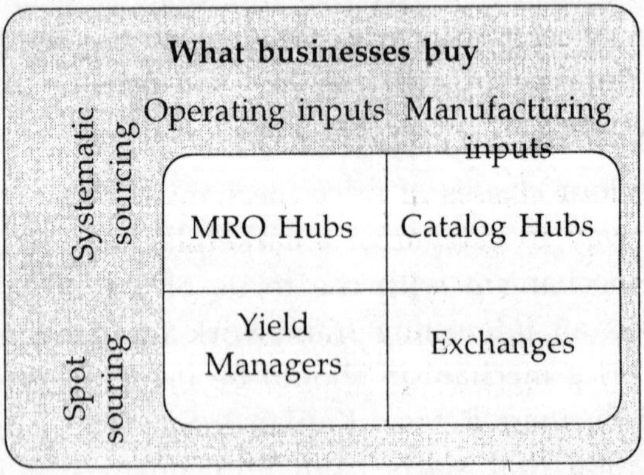

Figure 3: The B2B Matrix

Catalog Hubs: The difference between emarketplaces in this category and those in the past one, is that emarketplaces that are Catalog Hubs are vertical. The products are often more valuable but are still sold at list prices and within pre-negotiated contracts.

Yield Managers: These emarketplaces are horizontal and provide common operating resources like transportation and manufacturing capacity, which enable companies to manage temporary workload peaks. Also buying and selling of excess capacity such as general manpower is included.

Exchanges: Exchanges maintain relationships with the business participators so that they can conduct business without negotiating contracts or conditions. The goods and services handled by these emarketplaces are manufacturing inputs and the pricing mechanism is as the exchange model described earlier.

Functions supported by an emarketplace

To attract customers to an emarketplace, the emarketplace must create enough value for the customer in order to make a change from the traditional channel advantageous. In industries where it is hard for an emarketplace to compete with price, the additional services to the core products are important. The additional services which promote a deeper cooperation between companies will be of substantial importance for the emarketplaces, something that holds for public as well as for private emarketplaces. However, there is a risk when adding too many additional services to an emarketplace, especially to a vertical one. The added services have to be adapted for the customers and they have to be services which the customers demand. Besides, there is always a balancing between the cost of implementing a certain function and the added value for the participators. An emarketplace with too many additional services and products can be hard to navigate and it can be difficult to manage and gain profit from a too diversified marketplace. Strategies like supporting all customers in all processes are receipts for failure.

Furthermore, some activities such as demonstration, testing and persuasion might be handled less efficiently at an emarketplace than by for example a physical sales force. Some activities that might be handled at an emarketplace are mapped according to their business impact and ease of implementation. Functions like ordering, order status, pricing, online configuration etc. are functions which affect the companies' businesses substantially and, at the same time, are comparatively effortless to implement.

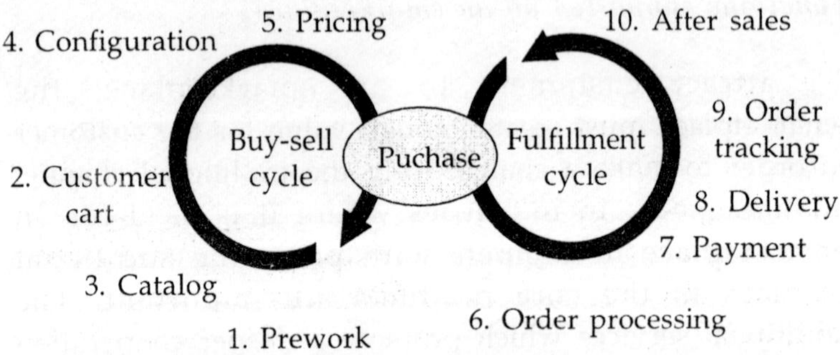

Figure 4: Activities in Internet purchase divided into two cycles

The ordering is one of the best functions suited to handle online. The companies can save a considerable amount of resources in their order processes if these processes are handled by an emarketplace. Even in the best companies up to 20 percent of all orders and invoices contain at least one error, a figure that can decrease down to less than one percent with help of online logistics. Besides, the author states, lead-times in the distribution process typically drop significantly.

Important functions in order to add value for the participating parties Gartner Group has developed a trade model of how purchases are conducted on the Internet. The model is divided into two parts. The first part is a buy-sell cycle in which the customers find products that meet their needs. The buy-sell cycle culminates in a purchase and is followed by a fulfillment cycle which includes activities from order processing and payment to delivery and after sales. In order to provide an online purchase service valuable for the customers, as many as possible of these activities have to be covered by the service.

Content Manager

To facilitate selection of product and supplier the emarketplace has to show the products and services sold in a way that lets the customer search by product, price, capacity etc. Since the data in the product catalog changes continuously, routines for updating have to be settled as well. If several suppliers are tied to the marketplace different strategies for displaying the goods and services might have to be used. For example, some suppliers might not want all customers to see all products or prices, suppliers might want to have their product catalog behind their own network's firewalls etc.

Configurators

If the customer decides to buy a product, the customer might need help to get the right version of the product etc. In order to be able to deliver more sophisticated and customized products and services than MRO commodities online, organizations have to implement some sorts of configurators. Any business segment in which internal expertise is used to make product and solutions recommendations may have advantages from configuration tools.

Aberdeen presents a division of the configurators based upon the primary users of the configurator. While the product configurators are used by the in-house engineering and manufacturing departments in order to ensure that the components in a product are compatible with each other, sales and external sales configurators are used later in the products flow.

A well functioning sales or external sales configurator may help the sales organizations or even the end-customers to place correct orders that fulfill the end-customers' needs.

Requisition routing and approval

After the customers have chosen and configured products, the fulfillment cycle as presented in Figure 4 starts. The first activity is order processing. Most companies have certain policies for which roles are allowed to process orders. When starting with e-business there might be a risk that more employees begin to order products themselves instead of via the traditional internal channels. Emarketplaces with functionality to route requisitions to the appropriate managers for their approval can have advantages since they support the customers in their purchasing process and force the user to follow correct purchasing routines.

Settlement

The emarketplaces have to handle the payment in some way. This can be solved by letting a third party take care of this function, by implementing a standardized payment solution or by building proprietary routines within the company.

Fulfillment

The fulfillment is the most complicated part for an emarketplace to handle, but also the part where the largest savings can be found. After the order has been matched with one of the previously described price mechanisms, a complex series of events set off which lead to delivery of the product. Mainly about physical goods and the consequences they lead to. The hard part is to handle all exceptions that can occur, for example out of stock, incorrect orders etc. The customers want the ability to track orders as well as seeing information about inventory, delivery times and production capacity and they want to have this information in real time.

Many emarketplaces send orders to the suppliers and leave the remainder of the fulfillment to the trading parties, which often handle these parts of the purchase offline. This is due to the fact that the emarketplaces usually are not integrated tightly enough with the supplier's back-office systems and the fact that these systems normally are not built with online ordering in mind and demand human interaction for handling incorrect orders and other exceptions.

It is of substantial importance that the emarketplace adds value for the participating parties. If not, it will be much harder to overcome the critical mass of participators needed to run the emarketplace. This might be particularly true in case of internal marketplaces. The added value can come in form of cut lead-times, lowered costs, better support, more information about the customer etc.

However, when reading about how the different types of e-business models add value to the participants, one must know what the authors have as a reference point. Is the point of reference an isolated company which only communicates with mail or is it a well functioning sales network with an efficient usage of information systems? Several of the below quoted authors, believe, compare with companies which, today, are not using information systems that coordinate them with the other participants in their network.

Added value for buyers

The substantial advantages buyers can get from e-business in form of price transparency, lowered search costs, wider selection etc. For example, buyers can use emarketplaces to focus their purchases of indirect material on preferred suppliers which they have pre-defined agreements with, or to take advantage of dynamic pricing mechanisms such as auction or exchange models.

— *Lower administrative costs:* With faster approvals and easier communication the cost of processing a purchase order can decrease substantially.

— *Control of maverick buying:* By channeling all approvals and funding through the procurement software buyers can control the maverick buying, e.g. buying outside permission or contracts.

— *End-to-end procurement cycle:* The electronic connections make it possible to tie the different parties' system together. For example, buyers can look in their suppliers systems to see inventory etc.

— *Buying consortiums:* By cooperating through an emarketplace small buyers can obtain the same price advantages that earlier was reserved for the large buyers. Furthermore, large companies with decentralized purchasing departments can benefit from coordinating their procurement to take advantage of their corporate purchasing power. In conclusion, the advantages for the buyers can be summarized into possibilities as lower costs for administration and supervising, increased control over the purchasing process and lower prices.

Added value for suppliers

The sellers are the most vulnerable participants on emarketplaces. There is a risk that the sellers have to compete on a more transparent market where the customers only search for low prices. Therefore, the strategy for the sellers is to set up seller-controlled emarketplaces unless the company gains substantially from lowered transaction costs or increased reach from joining a buyer-controlled or a neutral emarketplace.

However, sellers with their own emarketplace may have to open up their web site and invite competitors or at least complementors even if this means a decrease in sales in order to retain the control of the marketplace.

The substantial advantages may be found for sellers if the emarketplace ventures are handled correct. Possible advantages are for example:

— *Lower coordination costs:* As business partners move online, a potential exists to streamline the entire supply chain. Companies connecting with their customers and suppliers through an emarketplace can save costs and efforts by better coordination along the supply chain caused by better and faster information transmission.

— *Higher availability:* The supplier can increase the value experienced by the customer by increasing the availability.

— *Lower customer acquisition costs:* Suppliers can find new customers at a lower cost than earlier.

— *Lower selling cost:* Fewer errors, faster handling and lower inventory levels are possible effects of an emarketplace venture.

— *Some sellers will see higher prices:* Suppliers selling used goods or products with short life span can use emarketplaces with auction models and have a chance to get increased revenues for certain products. This since more interested buyers can be reached and that buyers willing to pay high prices can be found. In addition to constituting an additional sales channel, the emarketplaces, as seen above, may offer the supplier lower administrative cost, better coordination and the possibility to give the customer better support in form of faster supply handling and better information.

Choosing the right way to interact online

As seen during the explanation of different types of electronic hubs or emarketplaces, the choice of type differs depending on market position, overall strategy, market structure etc. In this section will briefly describe some additional factors that should help to decide the appropriate emarketplace strategy.

Berryman et al have compiled four questions companies should ask before they determine which strategy they should adopt. Are there transactions saving or benefits to be realized? Since cost reductions and increased process efficiency are two major reasons to join or start an emarketplace companies should conduct a detailed analysis of their current sales process.

If the most significant improvements are internal, the company should consider starting an internal e-hub to facilitate the processes. Apart from process improvements distribution of printed documents, product development, information management and wider reach might be categories where costs can be reduced or benefits found.

If there are substantial savings or benefits with an emarketplace for a certain product, the competitors are likely to set up own emarketplaces. This pressure from the surroundings can drive the company to an early presence, thus the competition can help the company getting out of the starting blocks. The developing speed of a market depends on the inefficiency of the current transactions and on how sophisticated the buyers are. Customer sophistication can be measured by their ability to place correct orders, understanding the differences between vendors, knowledge about the product etc.

This question is asked to determine which marketplace model that would be most effective. If the company's product is strongly branded and different from its competitors, the company might have better success opportunities if the product is sold from an own e-hub.

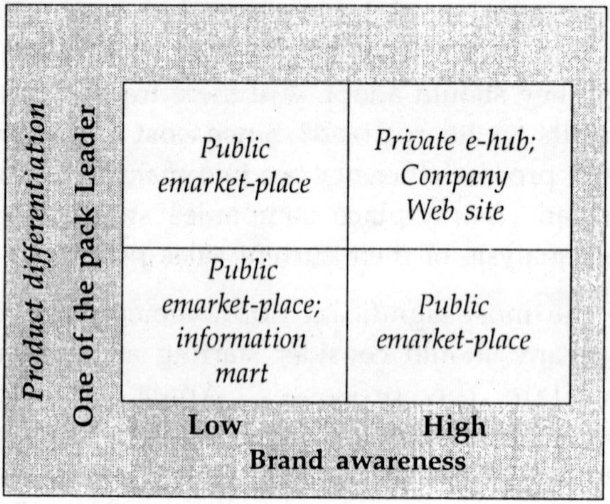

Figure 5: Choosing the right marketplace

Companies selling weaker products or selling products to a market with lower brand awareness should consider joining one or several external emarketplaces. Would a neutral intermediary be beneficial? Involving a third party in the emarketplace venture will, of course, lead to that the eventual profits have to be shared with an additional partaker. However, involving a neutral intermediary can bring positive effects such as more transactions, better service, more information about the customers and their purchase behavior and experience of earlier emarketplace ventures, advantages that might outweigh the drawbacks.

The two most important questions to be answered before deciding if and how emarketplaces should be used is first how the company should manage the change from traditional channels and, second, with which partners the company should get in alliance.

The second of these two questions is closely related to the last of the questions compiled by Berryman et al, while the first concerns something not covered by Berryman's et al questions. Finally, many authors state that traditional sales representatives even in the future will be the key to the buying process. Most suppliers will use emarketplaces as a complement to the traditional channels, rather then as a replacement for them. This because some product segments demand a detailed explanation, deep competence, and negotiation before a purchase. These products may be sold with direct sales contacts and then fulfilled via the emarketplace.

An e-hub is a comprehensive concept which includes public emarketplaces with numerous suppliers and buyers as well as internal marketplaces within a single company aimed to facilitate that company's processes. It is not totally clear what all authors include in their definition of emarketplaces and will therefore use the term electronic hub when talking about internal emarketplaces.

An important point of origin for companies at all times has been their relation to other companies. The individual firm is only a part of a more widespread network of suppliers, intermediaries, distributors and companies selling competing or complementing products and services. This makes it hard to study a company or unit within a company without looking at the company as a part of a larger network. In today's ever increasing competitive environment companies have to prove their right to exist by adding value with their products and services in an effective way. The companies have to focus on continuous improvements and customer satisfaction in order to keep their network position.

To be competitive and profitable over time all the company's value-added activities have to be efficient and coordinated. In 1985 Porter presented a model that segregates the company into a number of activities.The value-adding activities can, according to Porter, be divided into primary activities that are involved in the creation, sales and transfer of the product and support activities that supports the primary ones.

To make the activities as efficient as possible it is important to build linkages between them, both horizontal linkages between primary activities and vertical connections between primary and the supporting activities. For example, the inbound logistics department and the operations department could use a common information system in order to get the purchases done just in time. Linkages also exist between companies, the individual value chain is only a link in a wider value system. How suppliers or buyers perform their activities affect the performance and cost of the activities within the particular firm. By coordinating the suppliers' and the buyers' activities with the ones inside the own firm, all parties can gain considerable advantages.

Virtual value chain

The value chain can be extended in a number of ways. The complement Porter's value chain with a virtual one. While the traditional value chain treats information as a supporting element the virtual value chain model sees information as a source that can add value. That companies should create value by gathering, organizing, selecting, synthesizing and finally distributing the information to the customers.

By doing these five steps the company can create new markets, products and services. Thus, using the virtual value chain highlights the fact that information adds value for the customer. Besides, by collecting and sharing information with the adjacent actors the company can tie tighter relationships and achieve better coordination.

Value networks

The value chain is an important tool in order to break up the individual company into its activities. This is vital since participants conducting the independent activities they are best at ideally form a network. The companies within the networks build more or less tight relationship to each other. Hammarkvist et al have categorized these into: technical relationships, relationships in terms of time, knowledge relationships, social relationships, economical relationships and legal relationships. The bonds facilitate sharing of information within the network and give the participating companies a stability that can lead to a common ambition of development. Areas where networks supported by different forms of information technology add substantial advantages such as

Coverage: The customers can be offered all products and services they need from one single source. This source can coordinate the other participants in the network in a way that shapes an entirety for the customer.

Focusing: By being a part of a network that can offer a wide range of products and services the individual firm can focus on the things they are doing best. If every company in the network focus on their core business the network as a whole can be more efficient.

Process efficiency: To keep their place in the network the companies have to focus on continuously improving their processes. These individual improvements often benefit the whole network.

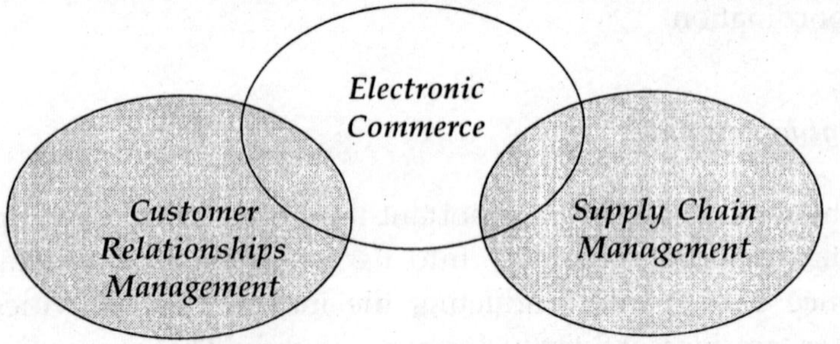

There are three different aspects that companies should focus on in order to improve their networks' positions. These aspects are:

Customer Relationship Management (CRM), Electronic Commerce and Supply Chain Management (SCM): These three areas can, in one way or another, help companies tighten their relations and increase the value of their network positions. The three aspects overlay each other and can be hard to distinguish from each other. For example, both Supply Chain Management and Customer Relationship management have been strongly affected and improved by electronic commerce. Electronic commerce can help joining supply chain management and customer relationship management to an entirety beneficial for the whole business network.

Supply chain management

Even if the definition of Supply Chain Management differs slightly among authors, most authors seem to agree that the concept considers the economic functions of the entire supply chain, from the suppliers of raw materials to the end-customers. Starting with the needs of its customers, a company must analyze how its supply chain is enabling or hindering its efforts to meet those needs. Firms must identify high-value opportunities for improvement through partnership, value-managed relationships or vertical integration. The differences between Supply Chain Management and other channel relationship theories are for example the amount of mutual sharing and monitoring of information and the amount of coordination of multiple levels in the channel.

The Internet is not only simplifying the distribution of information and the possibilities for a closer relationship with the customers and the suppliers. It also highlights the whole supply chain. Suddenly, all participants can see what the different links in the chain are doing and what they are costing. This will lead to that some middlemen disappear while others, who are doing the job better, appear. The supply chain will be reworked in many industries and become more Internet driven.

Three major issues that need to be considered when analyzing supply chain problems are: The flow of products. It is important to map the supply chain as far as to the end-customer. This because it is the end-customer with its purchase process that starts the activities in the supply chain. Moreover, it is possible that difficulties for the final customer may arise between the last organization in the chain and the actual use of the product.

The information flows: Many authors describe the flow of information as the critical key to effective supply chain operations. Thus, the entire channel can be managed more efficiently if its members have access to information relevant for the conduction of their business. However, it is not necessary that all chain members have the same information, as long as they get the information needed for them to conduct their own business better. By having an effective information flow within the supply chain the flow of material through the supply chain can be considerably smoother.

The organization and structure of the supply chain. It is of significant importance that the relationships within the supply chain serve as value adders and do not deteriorate the flow of products or information. There are several strategies for which channels that should be used to reach the end-customers. Whichever chosen the value-adding aspect has to be taken in consideration.

Customer Relationship Management

While Supply Chain Management focus on flows, Customer Relationship Management presents a distinctive relationship perspective. The term is widely used and there is no common definition but roughly all activities for coordinating, consolidating and integrating an enterprise's points of contact with their customers, partners and suppliers can be called Customer Relationship Management. Companies knowing their customers and their preferences can design offers where products, services and sales channels are adjusted to suit the particular customer or segment of customers.

Marketing, sales and service are three main areas for CRM. In each of these three areas companies have to develop different specific CRM capabilities such as 'measuring marketing effectiveness' and 'executing effective marketing plans' in marketing. In sales 'developing and executing an effective channel strategy,' and 'measuring sales effectiveness' are two important capabilities and finally in service and after-sale activities 'understanding customer profitability and cost to serve,' and 'developing differentiated/tiered customer service' are activities the companies should be able to handle. A study by Andersen Consulting showed that companies with specific CRM strategies enjoy better financial performance, similar evidences. To build the foundation for profitability it is important that the whole supply chain focuses on and supports activities to maintain long-term relations with the customers. The use of information technology has increased the possibilities for sharing customer information among channel partners.

The information technology has also made companies move away from market and product centricity towards a complete realignment of business processes in order to integrate with customer processes, which creates additional value to the customer and finally leads to lasting customer relations. In order to achieve this, many companies have begun to build their organizations around customer service and markets instead of around products or divisions. In a presentation of CRM, the maximization of customer value is about understanding the chain that builds a long-term customer relationship. Their model consists of four phases that the customer goes through during a purchase and activities that the selling company can perform to support this.

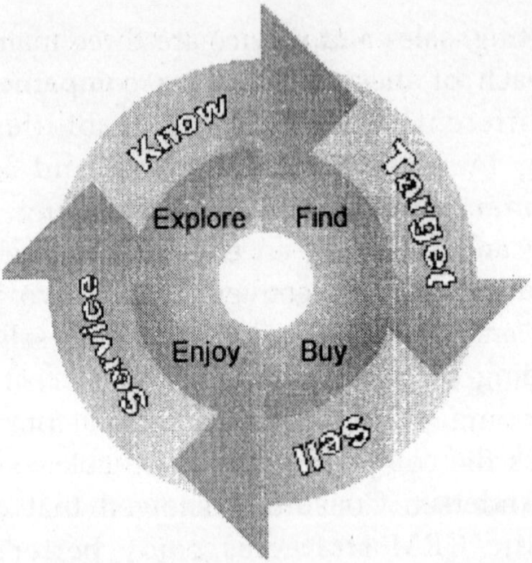

Figure 6: Activities for building a long customer relationship

During the explore phase the customer expresses a need and search for a suitable product. The more the selling company knows about their customer the better information can be presented to the customer. In the following find phase the customer finds and evaluates the product, here the selling company can differentiate their offer so it suits the customer. When this phase is concluded the customer hopefully buys the product. If the sales channel is designed in a suitable way this chance increases. Finally the customer enjoys the purchase and wants adequate service and support.

To support this process the different parties have to get suitable aids. In the following section assisting entities which support the activities in the process will be presented shortly.

Know: Information from databases with customer data, market analysis etc.

Target: For example electronic presence on the Internet designed in a way that makes it possible for the customers to adjust products and services according to their needs.

Sell: Effective sales and distribution channels designed to suit if not all so at least the most important customers.

Service: Order routines, saved information about the customers' earlier questions, systems and buys.

Channel Management

Much work has been done to enhance internal operations while the channels themselves have been somewhat neglected. This implies that managing the supply channels in a beneficiary way should be an excellent way to increase profits and competitiveness. The rapid information technology developments have given channel evolution a valuable boost. The Internet will challenge the present middle role between manufacturer and customer in the channel. However, as many authors claim this does not automatically lead to the death of the middlemen. Instead many new opportunities arise for intermediaries in the new information era. Moreover, using the Internet does not necessarily mean that all other channels will be abandoned. Many of the channels will coexist since they in many cases fulfill different customer needs.

The identified strategies for companies to reach their customers with help from the Internet. Three of these are:

Augment existing channels

Internet can enable companies to sell on markets or to customers that their existing channels are missing. With the augment existing channels strategy companies use the Internet as a new channel which complements their existing channels. The customers addressed by the Internet channel are not the same as them the existing channels address. The term virtualization and means that the additions to the channels mainly should serve well-informed and perceptive customers. However, this does not mean that intermediaries are cut out, merely that information is passed on more effectively in the supply chain. By using the Internet, companies can reach markets that are too fragmented and expensive to serve with a traditional outside sales force.

Enable existing channels for e-commerce

For many companies with existing sales channels, it can be hard to replace them with new electronic channels. Moreover, for many companies their customers are best served with their existing sales channels. The existing sales force has valuable information about the customers, support and configuration etc. Companies using this enabling strategy try to implement an e-commerce solution which affects the entire channel all the way to the end-customer, although not overriding it. The solution should support the sales process and information processes all through the channel. A similar strategy when they present their 'providing value-added services'-strategy. In this strategy, retailers act more like information or service brokers. Their focus shift from distribution to information gathering. This will make them vital in the supply chain again even after the traditional distribution role has become commoditized.

Disintermediate the channel

A technology forecaster at the Institute for the Future explains disintermediation such as "...networks and information systems [that] will allow buyer and seller to interact directly, thereby eliminating intermediaries and radically shortening value chains". They claim that it is about redefining or unbundling the channel partners' roles. More clear definition; they argue that disintermediation is when a certain stage in the supply chain is overridden. Companies that initiate this strategy will have problems with their existing channels since this strategy's aim is to eliminate the middlemen.

Today many companies' intermediaries have substantial control over the customer since they traditionally have had all contact with the customers and have lot of information about the buyer's needs and preferences. Meeker & Phillips believe that there are a number of factors that have to be considered before overriding an intermediary step in the supply chain. There is a difference between service and manufacturing industry. While the producers of physical products always will have to deal with shipment and inventory problems, the service industry does not suffer from these difficulties.

The implies that intermediaries in the service industry are the ones that most likely will be disintermediated. The more digitizable the product is the greater the possibilities for disintermediation are. However, the financial services sector has shown that IT alone will not automatically lead to disintermediation. The several other important factors, such as the current strength of the middlemen that will affect the possibilities for disintermediation. However, if the company succeeds with eliminating companies in the supply chain that do not add value, large savings can be achieved and considerable knowledge about the customers might be obtained.

Strategic channel phases

There is a general trend towards reintermediation. They do not identify this as an actual strategy, it is a development on the market. Reintermediation is when the group of previously disintermediated organizations are able to come back in the supply chain. The Internet will lead to a market development in a number of different phases. Before Internets breakthrough in an industry, very few middlemen only using the Internet to reach its customers exist.

As the industry mature, more intermediaries use only e-commerce in their sales, which leads to a disintermediation phase where the traditional intermediaries are losing the majority of the market they are serving to the ones using Internet as a sales tool. It is possible for the traditional intermediaries to take back parts of the market share lost to the e-commerce-only middlemen by becoming e-commerce-able intermediaries, i.e. able to perform electronic commerce themselves, perhaps on markets previously not served by them. It is not necessarily the samē company as the one that has been disintermediated that retakes market share from the e-commerce-only companies. Moreover, traditional intermediaries can also benefit from the reintermediation phase by providing new value-adding services, unrelated to their previous core business. New companies can also benefit from the reintermediation phase and, for example, become information brokers. The e-commerce-only intermediaries can also gain profits from becoming a technology provider to the existing companies, something that might be more profitable than being intermediaries themselves. Some of the factors explain reintermediation are:

Ownership of co-specialized assets: The area-specific expertise, installed customer base and supplier relationships enhance the existing companies chances to implement a successful new strategy. It is more unlikely that an e-commerce only intermediary, i.e. only doing business online, will have these competitive advantages than a traditional intermediary will.

Economies of scale: E-commerce only intermediaries have to build up a large amount of customers from scratch while the traditional companies already have a large customer base. While new intermediaries have to work hard in order to get the necessary economies of scale, traditional companies start off ahead with, hopefully, enough customers to begin with. The overall goal is to minimize the transaction cost per customer something that might be very costly for new intermediaries. However, these companies will have a first mover competitive advantage, which might be crucial in order to get support from the market.

The different strategic phases because it is not obvious that they consider it possible for a company to use many different channels. Although a certain channel, e.g. a channel serving a specific segment of the customers, might reach the reintermediation phase other channels, served by the same company, might continue to stay in the intermediation or disintermediation phase in the foreseeable future. Furthermore, point out that there still is a possibility for new intermediaries to continue to enter the business arena with the help of the Internet as a part of the reintermediation phase. The group of traditional intermediaries will have the dominant market share, but perhaps not where their traditional core business has been.

Channel Conflicts

Channel conflicts usually occur when two or more intermediaries try to reach parts of the same customer segment. However, this is not necessarily a bad thing since it can force non-rational intermediaries to change or leave the channel. Dangerous conflicts for the producer on the other hand typically occur when one effective channel targets a segment already served by another effective intermediary in another of the company's distribution channels. It is important to point out that channel conflicts are not exclusively between companies, different channels within a single business group may cannibalize on each other as well as on external channels. Made a framework for analyzing when channel conflicts are potentially dangerous and what decisions to make given certain situations. If a dangerous channel conflict has developed, much attention must be devoted to it in order to resolve the crisis.

Lambe states that there are four strategies for resolving channel conflicts:

Negotiation: Discussions aimed at resolving the crisis. The negotiating parties can either bargain with each other or focus on problem solving. There are two types of negotiation strategies that the parties can choose which will affect the relationship in the channel in very different ways:

Predatory: Channel members using this strategy assume that there is a fixed economic value between the companies where the channel conflict occurs, i.e. only one company can benefit from the negotiation. Therefore this player does not care about the other party's needs.

Symbiotic: Channel members using this strategy believe that there are economic benefits from cooperation, i.e. both companies might end up better off. Consequently, these organizations try to help the other party too. This is a problematic situation since both parties benefit the most when being predatory if the other party is using the symbiotic strategy. However, the predatory-predatory situation is the worst possible scenario for both companies, although the superior strength of a company might make this strategy the easiest to adopt and carry through.

Persuasive mechanism: One channel member influences the other participant's behavior. This requires a great deal of trust between the two parties since it is usually very hard to convince a hostile opponent to take view.

Legal remedies: Use of legal methods, e.g. contracts or laws, to persuade the channel member to convert to the organization's view. This should only be used as a last resort since using legal remedies generally is one of the best ways to destroy business relationships.

Climate management: The interactions of boundary personnel over an extended period of time determine the channel climate. Climate management is in essence to prevent conflicts by developing a positive channel climate over time. Conflicts do not normally appear overnight and much effort can be spared if it is detected and prevented at an early stage. Relationship marketing ethics will help people in the value chain to implement a positive channel climate.

The channel conflict is inevitable but that it is not always as dangerous as one thinks. Therefore, it is necessary to analyze the conflicts in order to find out which ones are dangerous and worth concentrating on. Channel conflicts often are good since they force the participants in the channel to improve their business in order to retain their positions. However, if the channel's participants begin to fight for accounts, the result can be a price war between the internal units in the channel which seldom is good for any channel member.

Buying and selling digital products

The Internet has opened new possibilities for distribution of digital products such as software, articles, music or images to customers over the whole world at a very low cost. The Internet plays the role of distribution medium in the case of digital products and he thinks that the range of digital products will expand substantially with the growth of e-business.

There are several differences between digital and physical products. The maybe most significant difference concerns properties that determine how the products are produced and distributed. The fact that the variable cost of producing another copy of a digital product does not increase, even if the number of copies is very large, is unique. Other special properties are:

The digital products are costly to produce but cheap to reproduce: When the first copy is produced, most costs are sunk costs. There are no natural capacity limits or bottlenecks in the reproduction apart from cheap reproduction, distribution of digital products is also inexpensive. A strategic implication of low reproduction and distribution costs is that it makes it possible to give away product samples at zero or to a relatively small extra cost. However, then one has to face the problem of controlling what the customer can try without having to charge them. Selling a bundle of many distinct information goods for a single price often yields higher profits and greater efficiency than selling the same goods separately. The reasons are for example that the bundled products can be tested to work together, the price taken for the bundled package can be higher than the average price when selling the products separately, a reduction in buyer diversity can decrease the development costs etc. Furthermore, concluded that product bundling is controlled by different relative costs as follows:

Production cost: The margin cost of producing another unit which is incorporated in the bundle.

Transaction and distribution cost: The total costs of shipping including administrative work and costs related to the payments attached with the bundle. Binding cost. The cost of setting up the bundle i.e. making changes in format to facilitate the distribution of the items as a bundle.

Menu cost: The cost of handling a multitude of prices. The choice of items in the bundle may be very large making the number of possible bundles even larger that may all be priced differently. However, bundling may also reduce the possibilities for different prices by reducing the total amount of product offerings. The primary reason for bundling is to increase the total revenues from the sales instead of having a cost focus. This is mainly connected to the dispersion in perceived customer value, the perceived value of the bundle often is less diverse than the perceived value of the individual products. This could instead imply that bundling will increase in the future.

Selling digital products online

A framework for deciding which products are most suitable for electronic commerce given a certain business type. The authors state that digital products and services together have the greatest market potential and the least business risk to be sold online. This is mainly explained by benefits gained from the logistical advantages of digital products. An explosive development of digital products and they forecast that the Internet will be the dominating market channel for these products. The reason for this depends not only on the smooth delivery but also of added value from interaction with the customer and new pricing models. Digital products can be bought in form of licenses or keys. For example, a company can buy the right to use Microsoft Excel at an additional computer on its network without having to buy the whole program but just a license. Furthermore, software or music can be bought for the particular time it is used by the customer. It is possible to buy the right to listen to a MP3 song once.

These ways of purchasing may lead to that the number of small purchases increases substantially. To keep the lead-times for this small, frequent buys at a decent level, selling them online with instant delivery might be the way most companies chose. Other authors are not as sure that the Internet is the only or best way of shipping information goods. Providers of proprietary information should keep existing direct channels in addition to an Internet presence. However, the number of steps between the production and delivery of especially digital goods and services will decrease since the producer now can distribute their products on the Internet in a much easier way. Instead of just measuring the suitableness of electronic commerce from the market potential and business risk/logistics importance, Brehmer classifies products into four dimensions. These four dimension do not cover market potential but judge how easy it is to sell the products online. The four dimensions are:

Information-intensity: How much information does the customer need to gather in the entire buying process?

Multisensory appeal: To what extent does the product evaluation require customers to engage the senses of smell, taste and touch?

Atmospherics: How important is the role of the physical store environment and the interaction with the salesperson in the purchase process?

Logistical efficiency: How efficiently can the product be packaged and shipped to individual customers?

Digital products excellently fulfill the last of these four dimensions. This since the products in many cases is produced, or reproduced, at the same time as they are ordered. Since buying digital products rarely demands that the buyer engages his/her senses, these products also seem to be suitable concerning the second dimension. However, digital products in the form of software is often very complex, much information might have to be transferred between the supplier and buyer in order to identify the customer's needs and to describe the product. This may speak against selling advanced software online or, at least, means that the supplier has to know the customer and its needs.

Procurement process

In order to sell and distribute products and services to its customer a company has to understand the customers' procurement processes. This is of course also valid for digital products. If consideration is not taken to how the customers are buying there is a substantial risk that new ventures will be unprofitable or at least less successful than predicted. This is especially significant when introducing new sales or distribution channels. Important things for the selling company to know are for example how purchasing decisions are made, how orders are coordinated and which persons that have to attest the orders. Depending on what author one reads, the definition of the procurement process can differ substantially. However, stages in the procurement process which many authors have in common are: define need, select product and supplier, order, transaction and payment.

The transaction phase, on which this thesis will focus, contains attest, order, order confirmation, delivery and payment. There are several ways in which e-commerce can simplify this second phase, for example by providing better information and a foundation for better supervision. The procurement process within a company can differ substantially depending on the product purchased. The procurement process into two dimensions, the complexity of the product and how often the product is bought. There are significant differences in buying behavior depending of these dimensions.

Buying complex products

When more complex products are bought, more persons from different hierarchical levels are involved as well as more company functions. There are three different roles involved in the purchase:

Executors: Take care of most activities to drive the process forward, office administrators can for example take responsibility for this role.

Determinators: Existing or potential users involved in key decision phases, the executors prepare the information needed while the determinators decide what to do. High level managers often have this role.

Gatekeepers: All categories of roles can serve as gatekeepers. However, only the executors are normally perceived by the selling company as gatekeepers. The gatekeepers act as interfaces for the customer towards the supplier. When buying complex products, the determinators are especially powerful during the first phases when the products are evaluated and a decision is made while the executors is doing the time-consuming following steps. The division of the tasks is due to the fact that the complexity of the products requires more time and knowledge than the determinators possibly can devote to every single product in Phase 2. The executors are often specialized on a certain product, which make them more suitable to handle the practical issues.

A consequence of this is that the executors become more powerful in the purchasing of complex products because of their knowledge and availability of time. However, that what is considered complex is highly personal and depends upon a number of factors such as experience and education. The main differences in activities are, when buying complex products more qualitative analysis and more technical negotiations are performed. The qualitative analysis contains an investigation of which customer needs that the product can fulfill. When less complex products are bought the specific needs are more obvious and a separate analysis is therefore unnecessary. For example, technical negotiations arise when the buyer has a problem and invites a supplier to discuss this problem. Sometimes the supplier can offer the customers unique products or solutions or can recommend products not known to the customer. These types of negotiations can be a necessity since the buyer in some cases does not have enough knowledge to determine what to order to fill the customers needs.

Selling complex products

Companies selling complex products must have routines for how support should be given to the buyers during the whole procurement process and not just in the decision phase. Moreover, the selling company has to know how to present information for the customers' decision-makers in an appropriate way since they often do not have detailed knowledge of differences between similar complex products. The appearance of the distribution channel between the suppliers and buyers is highly determined by product complexity. They argue that up until now, mainly simple products such as books and music CDs have been sold on electronic marketplaces. The authors mean that two factors, asset specificity and product complexity control what the structure between buyers and seller looks like.

Asset specificity: A list of seven types of asset specificities that should be considered when determining the products' properties. These are: site specificity, physical asset specificity, human asset specificity, dedicated assets, brand name capital, temporal specificity and finally time specificity.

Complexity of product description: Complexity of product description is defined as 'the amount of information needed to specify the attributes of a product in enough detail to allow potential buyers (whether producers acquiring production inputs or consumers acquiring goods) to make a selection'.

Products with low asset specificity and low product description complexity are likely to be sold at a traditional market with many buyers and sellers. However, if both factors are higher the authors claim that a single or a few sellers are likely instead of a market consisting of several sellers. Information technology can help to lower the complexity of the product description, but this is something that just recently has been learned by companies.

EDI has been used for decades, the aspects that might do the topic particularly interesting now is the decrease of cost for using electronic connections thanks to the expansion of the Internet. Other important developments from the pure EDI connections are that it has been easier to present information and to interact with other parties. More and more companies have begun to use the Internet in their purchase, sales and distribution. In order to increase volumes, find new markets or customers some companies have started electronic hubs where participators can interact online. These electronic marketplaces can either be private, inside an individual company, helping the units within the business group cooperate and be more effective, or public where many different companies can buy and sell products. The private ones are nearly exclusive for large global companies divided into different subsidiaries or units. Public electronic marketplaces on the other hand can help small companies reach a larger market or help large companies sell to small ones by aggregating orders. Whether private or not, several sellers and buyers interact on an electronic marketplace, even if these belong to the same business group in the private case.

In order to add value for the participating parties the emarketplaces must have more additional functions than just bringing buyers and suppliers together. Apart from being able to handle requisition routing, approval, fulfillment and settlement, it is important that the emarketplace can show the products and services sold in a way that makes it easy for the buyer to browse through the catalog as well as to search for specific properties. Other ways of providing added value are to have additional services, for example financing, credit, insurance and transportation.

The advantages of emarketplaces for the buyers can be summarized in lower costs for administration and supervising and better control over the purchasing process and in some cases lower prices. For the suppliers the emarketplaces can offer an additional sales channel, lower administration cost, better coordination and the possibility to offer the customer rapid order handling and better information. One must know the reference point when talking about the potential advantages with all e-business ventures. In this thesis, the point of reference is a company which is not using information systems that coordinate the company with the other participants in their network in an efficient way.

The emarketplaces can be categorized in a number of ways depending on ownership, focus etc. Different categories have their specific advantages and disadvantages. Depending on the market structure where the emarketplace will act, different categories of emarketplaces suit best.

Networks are considered increasingly important in today's economy. From Porters' original value chain model many discussions have arisen. One is the point of the virtual value chain where information is considered much more important than in the original model. The networks are built up in order to enhance business, this could be in form of coverage, focus or process efficiencies. Some authors believe that there are three components that companies should focus on to improve their networks: Supply Chain Management, electronic commerce and Customer Relationships Management. Supply Chain Management concerns all activities for delivering products to the end-customer as effectively as possible. That means that the company has to focus on activities around product flows, information flows and the organization that affect the companies supply chain.

The Internet has given many new possibilities for information sharing and lead to greater cost and information transparency throughout the supply chain.

Customer Relationship Management (CRM) on the other hand focuses on relationships instead of flows. There does not exist any unambiguous definition of CRM but many authors argue that it at least consist of marketing, sales and service. The Internet has made information sharing easier, which has led to possibilities for adapting the companies' processes to its customers' processes. This is important in order to maintain long and profitable relationships with customers, which is the goal of CRM. When using e-business at least three different channel strategies exist: augment existing channels, enable existing channels for e-commerce and disintermediate the channel, i.e. overriding existing channels.

The disintermediated channels will be reintermediated, i.e. formerly bypassed types of middlemen recover market share or take shares on markets previously not served by them. When channels are changing as drastically as it is expected that the Internet will force them to, there are risks of channel conflicts. However, not all channel conflicts are bad and therefore it is necessary to analyze what type of conflict really has occurred or will occur in order to judge what steps that are necessary to take. These steps are a mix of the possible strategies for resolving channel conflicts: negotiations, persuasive mechanisms, legal remedies and climate management.

Information goods in the frame of reference is that digital products indeed are different from other types of products. The key differences from physical products are:

The marginal production cost is zero, or close to zero: The distribution costs tend towards zero, at least the variable part of the costs These properties should be considered when strategies for marketing, selling and buying these products are developed. The product itself may consist of different components that are bundled together. Some authors believe bundling is the future of software products while other regards the Internet as something working against this phenomenon.

Buying can be separated into two dimensions: product complexity and how frequently the product is purchased. When buying complex products the actual purchaser, the so-called executor, becomes more important since that person has specific important knowledge about the products which people on higher positions do not posses. Therefore, larger companies which have specific departments dedicated to purchasing advanced products often can handle more of the purchase process themselves. Besides, the more technical competence the company possesses the easier the buying of complex products is.

Product complexity in two dimensions, asset specificity and complexity of product description. Furthermore, products that have low asset specificity and that are easy to describe are the most likely to be traded by many buyers and sellers on an open market. On the other hand, products with high asset specificity and complexity of description are more likely to be sold by one or a few sellers.

Advertising on the Internet

There are many rules that apply the forms of advertising on electronic marketing. These rules and guidelines protect businesses and consumers - and help maintain the credibility of the Internet as an advertising medium. The Federal Trade Commission (FTC) has prepared this guide to give you an overview of some of the laws it enforces. The Federal Trade Commission Act allows the FTC to act in the interest of all consumers to prevent deceptive and unfair acts or practices. In interpreting Section 5 of the Act, the Commission has determined that a representation, omission or practice is deceptive if it is likely to:

— mislead consumers and

— affect consumers' behavior or decisions about the product or service.

In addition, an act or practice is unfair if the injury it causes, or is likely to cause, is:

— substantial

— not outweighed by other benefits and

— not reasonably avoidable.

The FTC Act prohibits unfair or deceptive advertising in any medium. That is, advertising must tell the truth and not mislead consumers. A claim can be misleading if relevant information is left out or if the claim implies something that's not true. For example, a lease advertisement for an automobile that promotes "$0 Down" may be misleading if significant and undisclosed charges are due at lease signing. In addition, claims must be substantiated, especially when they concern health, safety, or performance. The type of evidence may depend on the product, the claims, and what experts believe necessary.

Sellers are responsible for claims they make about their products and services. Third parties - such as advertising agencies or website designers and catalog marketers - also may be liable for making or disseminating deceptive representations if they participate in the preparation or distribution of the advertising, or know about the deceptive claims. Advertising agencies or website designers are responsible for reviewing the information used to substantiate ad claims. They may not simply rely on an advertiser's assurance that the claims are substantiated.

In determining whether an ad agency should be held liable, the FTC looks at the extent of the agency's participation in the preparation of the challenged ad, and whether the agency knew or should have known that the ad included false or deceptive claims. To protect themselves, catalog marketers should ask for material to back up claims rather than repeat what the manufacturer says about the product. If the manufacturer doesn't come forward with proof or turns over proof that looks questionable, the catalog marketer should see a yellow "caution light" and proceed appropriately, especially when it comes to extravagant performance claims, health or weight loss promises, or earnings guarantees. In writing ad copy, catalogers should stick to claims that can be supported. Most important, catalog marketers should trust their instincts when a product sounds too good to be true.

Advertising directed to children raises special issues. That's because children may have greater difficulty evaluating advertising claims and understanding the nature of the information you provide. Sellers should take special care not to misrepresent a product or its performance when advertising to children.

The Children's Advertising Review Unit (CARU) of the Council of Better Business Bureaus has published specific guidelines for children's advertising that you may find helpful. The Internet provides unprecedented opportunities for the collection and sharing of information from and about consumers. But studies show that consumers have very strong concerns about the security and confidentiality of their personal information in the online marketplace. Many consumers also report being wary of engaging in online commerce, in part because they fear that their personal information can be misused. These consumer concerns present an opportunity for you to build on consumer trust by implementing effective voluntary industry-wide practices to protect consumers' information privacy.

The FTC has held a number of workshops for industry, consumer groups and privacy advocates to explore industry guidelines to protect consumers' privacy online. In June 1998, the FTC issued Online Privacy: A Report to Congress. The Report noted that while over 85 percent of all websites collected personal information from consumers, only 14 percent of the sites in the FTC's random sample of commercial websites provided any notice to consumers of the personal information they collect or how they use it.

While the 2000 survey showed significant improvement in the percent of websites that post at least some privacy disclosures, only 20 percent of the random sample sites were found to have implemented four fair information practices: notice, choice, access and security. Even when the survey looked at the percentage of sites implementing the two critical practices of notice and choice, only 41 percent of the random sample provided such privacy disclosures. The Children's Online Privacy Protection Act (COPPA) and the FTC's implementing Rule took effect April 21, 2000.

Commercial websites directed to children under 13 years old or general audience sites that have actual knowledge that they are collecting information from a child must obtain parental permission before collecting such information. Some FTC laws about specific marketing practices and the promotion of products and services in specific industries. The Franchise and Business Opportunity Rule requires franchise and business opportunity sellers to give consumers a detailed disclosure document at least 10 days before the consumer pays any money or legally commits to a purchase. The document must include:

— the names, addresses, and telephone numbers of other purchasers;

— a fully-audited financial statement of the seller;

— the background and experience of the business's key executives;

— the cost of starting and maintaining the business; and

— the responsibilities of the seller and purchaser once the purchase is made.

Multi-level marketing (MLM) also known as "network" or "matrix" marketing - is a way of selling goods and services through distributors. These plans typically promise that people who sign up as distributors will get commissions two ways - on their own sales and on the sales their recruits have made. Pyramid schemes - a form of multi-level marketing - involve paying commissions to distributors only for recruiting new distributors.

Pyramid schemes are illegal in most states because the plans inevitably collapse when no new distributors can be recruited. When a plan collapses, most people -

except those at the top of the pyramid - lose their money. MLMs should pay commissions for the retail sales of goods or services, not for recruiting new distributors. MLMs that involve the sale of business opportunities or franchises, as defined by the Franchise Rule, must comply with the Rule's requirements about disclosing the number and percentage of existing franchisees who have achieved the claimed results, as well as cautionary language.

The Truth in Lending Act requires creditors who deal with consumers to disclose information in writing about finance charges and related aspects of credit transactions, including finance charges expressed as an annual percentage rate. In addition, the Act establishes a three-day right of rescission in certain transactions involving the establishment of a security interest in the consumer's principal dwelling. The Act also establishes certain requirements for advertisers of credit terms. The Fair Credit Billing Act is important if you are a creditor billing customers for goods or services. The Act requires you to acknowledge consumer billing complaints promptly in writing and to investigate billing errors. The Act prohibits creditors from taking actions that adversely affect the consumer's credit standing until the investigation is completed, and affords other consumer protections during disputes. The Act also requires that creditors promptly post payments to the consumer's account, and either refund overpayments or credit them to the consumer's account. The Fair Credit Reporting Act requires that consumer reporting agencies (CRAs) - such as credit bureaus and resellers of consumer reports - that provide information to creditors, insurers, employers, and others, do so with due regard for the confidentiality, accuracy, and legitimate use of such data.

When those parties take adverse action on the basis of information in a credit report, they must identify the CRA that provided the report so that the consumer can learn how to get a copy to verify or contest its accuracy and completeness. Creditors and others may not knowingly provide false information to CRAs, which are required to maintain reasonable procedures to ensure the maximum possible accuracy of their data.

The Equal Credit Opportunity Act prohibits lenders from discriminating on the basis of race, color, religion, national origin, sex, marital status, age, receipt of public assistance income, or an applicant's good faith exercise of any rights under the Consumer Credit Protection Act. The ECOA requires creditors to provide applicants with the reasons credit was denied if the applicant asks. The Electronic Fund Transfer Act establishes the rights, liabilities, and responsibilities of participants in electronic fund transfer systems.

The EFTA requires participants to adopt certain practices when they deal with transaction accounting and preauthorized transfers and error resolution, and sets liability limits for losses caused by unauthorized transfers. The Consumer Leasing Act regulates personal property leases that exceed four months and are made to consumers for personal, family, or household purposes.

The statute requires that certain lease costs and terms be disclosed, imposes limitations on the size of penalties for delinquency or default and on the size of residual liabilities, and in some instances, requires certain disclosures in lease advertising. Advertisements promoting credit repair, promising loans for a fee in advance, or touting investment opportunities may trigger application of the FTC's Telemarketing Sales Rule if the ad allows consumers to order goods or services by telephone.

In general, this Rule does not apply to general media advertisements. If you're advertising credit repair, advance fee loans, or investment opportunities, or offering to recover money paid in previous telemarketing transactions, however, the Rule likely applies to you. Among other things, the Rule requires that certain disclosures be made before a customer pays for the goods or services. The Rule also prohibits material misrepresentations.

Testimonials and endorsements must reflect the typical experiences of consumers, unless the ad clearly and conspicuously states otherwise. A statement that not all consumers will get the same results is not enough to qualify a claim.

The Textile and Wool Acts require you to disclose country of origin information in catalogs and other mail order advertising and in Internet ads that sell textile and wool products. The description of each advertised item must include a statement that it was made in the U.S.A., imported or both. A general statement in your ads that all products are either made in the U.S.A. or imported is not adequate. Ads that say or imply anything about fiber content must disclose the generic fiber names in order of predominance by weight. This requirement applies to all ads, whether or not they solicit direct sales. The FTC works for the consumer to prevent fraudulent, deceptive and unfair business practices in the marketplace and to provide information to help consumers spot, stop and avoid them.

4

Electronic Cash Transactions

The emergence of electronic money (e-money) has prompted much research and study by both the public and private sectors. Although many have lauded the promise of these new payment methods for industry and government, less attention has been focused on the implications of e-money for consumers. Consumer acceptance in turn requires that consumers have confidence in the product; understand the benefits and risks of the new products; and believe that their concerns about the products have been considered and addressed.

The term 'e-money' encompasses a wide variety of existing and planned products designed to provide an alternative to traditional means of payment. This diversity of potential and existing e-money products makes it difficult to render a single description that encompasses all electronic money systems in terms of technological, market, or legal distinctions. For purposes of this programme, however, an 'e-money' or 'electronic stored-value' product is a prepaid balance of funds, or 'value,' recorded on a device controlled by the consumer, generally either a card or the consumer's personal computer. E-money can be used for point of sale or for

Internet-based purchases. The balance on the device is decreased, or debited, when the device is used for payment. A wide variety of card-based systems are possible, differing according to the technology used, whether the system is 'open' or 'closed,' whether transactions occur on-line to a central system or off-line, and whether the cards are disposable or reloadable. Card-based stored value has been in existence for many years. Early generations of card-based stored value, often known as pre-paid cards, involve recording a balance of funds on a magnetic stripe that is debited by the terminal after each use.

Although magnetic stripe technology provides a low-cost means to distribute stored value, it does not provide sufficient safety from tampering or counterfeiting to be applied to off-line systems in which relatively large amounts of value will be placed on the cards. In addition, options for reloading of magnetic cards are limited as is the ability to store transaction information. Smart cards, i.e., cards with an embedded microprocessor chip, provide features superior to those of magnetic stripe cards. The microprocessor chip can store and manipulate data according to pre-programmed functions on the chip and external instructions from a card-reading unit. Smart cards promise additional security by permitting sophisticated encryption technology to protect the value on the card from counterfeiting. In addition, smart cards may bundle various products on a single card, that could function as a credit card, a debit card, a stored value card, and a repository of personal information.

Many card-based systems presently in use are 'closed' systems—systems where the value is only redeemable in exchange for the issuer's goods or services. Most of these systems use magnetic stripe technology.

Common examples of closed systems include transportation systems in major metropolitan areas, photocopiers in public libraries, and long distance telephone cards. Utilities, laundry and parking facilities are also increasingly incorporating stored value systems. Other closed systems are multi-functional, and usually involve smart card technology. These systems generally involve a narrowly defined group of consumers, a small group of merchants, and a relatively small geographic area over which to install the necessary infrastructure. Such systems are also gaining in popularity. These semi-closed systems are most often seen on university and corporate campuses and surrounding environs, and on military installations. In truly open systems, on the other hand, e-money could be used with many merchants over an extended geographic area and function as a general medium of exchange.

Some stored-value card systems, such as pre-paid phone cards in the United States, interact with a central database system that maintains the records of funds associated with each card and require verification of every transaction on-line with the central system. However, most of the e-money systems envision that transactions will typically be off-line except for purposes of purchasing, reloading or redeeming the stored-value. Many of the current stored-value systems are reloadable, permitting consumers to add to the value on the cards through machines that accept currency or credit cards. Where cards are linked to the consumer's depository institution account, they can be reloaded through ATMs and in some cases through personal computers equipped with remote computer banking software and a card reader device.

A few e-money systems are designed primarily for Internet transactions, permitting consumers to use personal computers to make payments to other parties via Internet e-mail or other computer-to-computer communication methods. Consumers wishing to utilize these Internet systems must first install specialized software on their computers. In these systems, the device that stores the value is generally the consumer's personal computer rather than a card. The distinction between smart card and Internet based e-money systems appears to be diminishing as some providers of stored value cards are testing their systems internationally for Internet payments. Future systems may integrate these and other payment methods, possibly through the use of a smart card reader attached to the consumer's personal computer.

The Market for E-Money Products Consumers in the United States have a wide array of choices of payment mechanisms. They can use cash, checks, credit cards, debit cards, or money orders for many payments. Credit and debit cards are increasingly being accepted for smaller dollar payments—payments that traditionally were made in cash. Whether open e-money systems will succeed against this array of competing products in this market is unclear. Most retail payments in the US are made using one of six payment instruments: cash, checks, credit cards, debit cards, and Automated Clearing House ('ACH') debits and credits. The US has a predominantly paper-based payment system for retail transactions, relying on checks for 87 percent of noncash retail payments. The US is also the only developed country in which check use is increasing. Adoption of retail electronic payments has been relatively slow. However, there has been strong growth in electronic payments over the last several years as American consumers have become more familiar with these alternatives. For example, since 1990 consumers have increased their annual charge volume on bank credit cards by 128 percent. There has also been strong growth in the debit card market in recent years. Approximately 40 percent of financial consumers now use debit cards and the average number of monthly transactions grew from 4.7 to 7.3 in January of 1997. To date, e-money, whether card or Internet-based, remains a very minor player in the payments system.

E-money has been widely touted as an alternative to cash that provides consumers with added security and convenience for small-dollar transactions, while providing merchants greater efficiency in cash handling, and lower transaction fees. Although some have expressed doubts about the viability of e-money, these concerns have not stopped the proliferation of pilot programs worldwide. The major e-money sponsors are currently participating in pilot programs in Argentina, Australia, Brazil, Canada, Colombia, the Czech Republic, Hong Kong, Italy, Japan, Mexico, Norway, New Zealand, Poland, South Africa, Sweden, Switzerland and the United Kingdom. Additionally, Austria, China, Costa Rica, Greece, Israel, Korea, Malaysia, Moldova, the Netherlands, Saudi Arabia, and Singapore are also either presently or soon will be experimenting with domestic corporations' proprietary e-money products. Belgium, Denmark, Finland, France, Germany, Portugal, Spain, and Thailand have completed the experimentation stage and have begun implementing e-money systems nationwide. For example, Proton, founded by Banksys (a consortium of 60 banks), has issued 900,000 cards in Belgium alone, and more than 14 million cards worldwide. Several open e-money systems are currently in pilot phases in the United States. For example, over 1.7 million cards were produced at the 1996 Olympic Summer Games in Atlanta, and 200,000 transactions totaling about $1.1 million were conducted. Other pilot programmes currently underway in the US involve multipurpose multi-application smart cards that permit loyalty programs and ticketless airline travel.

One large-scale US pilot programme involving 50,000 consumers and over 500 merchants is currently underway on the Upper West Side of Manhattan. In this pilot, MasterCard and Mondex (in conjunction with Chase Manhattan Bank) and Visa (in conjunction with Citibank) in tandem are issuing their own products supported by interoperable readers capable of accepting value from either product. The results of these pilots to date indicate that consumer and merchant acceptance may be slower than initially thought. Internet-based e-money systems also promise consumers great convenience and security for Internet transactions. However, the development of the Secure Electronic Transactions protocol, encrypting consumer credit card numbers when used over the Internet, as well as the development of other security features for credit card transactions, may have satisfied consumers' desire for additional security in connection with an already-accepted payment mechanism. This development may cause Internet based e-money issuers to develop their product as a niche product for micro-payments, such as for purchases of information over the Internet. Additionally, as mentioned earlier, some stored value card issuers are exploring using their transaction protocols for Internet-based transactions.

Internet based e-money systems, however, have not yet been widely introduced or adopted by consumers or merchants. In fact, the three largest issuers of Internet payments products have conducted less than $3 million in transactions combined.

In addition to promising consumers greater convenience than cash, such products may also provide consumers greater physical security, particularly when consumers can add value to the cards at home using their personal computer. E-money will likely remain a minor segment of the US payments system for the near future. Consumers generally will not be compelled to use or accept e-money. Thus, issuers will face considerable market pressure to address factors that give rise to consumers' concerns in order to promote use of their products. Over time, advances in technology and decreasing costs in the storage of information should enable issuers to design stored value products with enhanced safety and security features that respond to consumers' demands. In addition, to promote use of their products, issuers will have an incentive to help consumers learn and become comfortable with the products through advertising, promotional campaigns, consumer education programmes.

E-money could also provide merchants the ability to reduce cash-handling costs, such as those resulting from employee theft. Additionally, some institutions with specialized needs are increasingly adopting stored value card systems. University campuses and their surrounding environs are one such specialized market. Universities, using smart card technology, can integrate payment capabilities with student identification cards, and provide students the convenience of only needing to carry one card. Other possible markets include corporate campuses, military installations and planned communities. For example, the US military is currently experimenting with stored value cards systems for their trainee's payroll. Government actions also may serve to help develop a larger market for e-money products. The Debt Collection Improvement Act of 1996 requires all federal government payments to be made via electronic means by 1999. The Financial Management Service currently anticipates delivering federal payments via direct deposit to all recipients with a deposit account at a financial institution.

Federal payment recipients who do not have a deposit account at a financial institution have the option of receiving electronic payments at an account established on their behalf by Treasury or if receiving an electronic deposit would be burdensome, recipients can exercise a hardship waiver and continue to receive paper checks by mail. Although e-money does not play an immediate role in the EFT' mandate, it may ultimately help eliminate government-issued, checks in the near future. Currently, traditional EFT payment mechanisms limit the government from making all payments electronically. For example, because direct deposit transactions require enrollment and authorization by the account holder well in advance of payment, the government must issue paper checks to individuals and businesses that require immediate payment.

E-money products could eliminate the necessity for paper checks in this situation by allowing the government to execute electronic payments immediately. Even now, some state governments are testing smart cards for the distribution of certain state administered benefits programs, such as food coupons and Women, Infants, and Children ("WIC") programs. Although the vast majority of these programs presently use on-line magnetic stripe cards, several states are exploring whether smart cards could be useful for the distribution of coupon-based benefit programs such as food stamps.

At the present time, the market for e-money is still developing, and it is difficult to predict its eventual structure. However, several important aspects of electronic money may affect the market's eventual development. E-money, like other electronic payment methods in use today, may display network characteristics, i.e. the value of the product to any user is increased as other potential users adopt the system. In particular, widespread e-money installation of point-of-sale devices capable of reading stored-value cards may be necessary to spur consumer demand while consumers may not demand stored value cards unless there are sufficient locations to use them. Conversely, merchants may lack the incentives to deploy terminals capable of accepting stored value cards unless consumers appear to be willing to use that payment mechanism.

Additionally, the technologies themselves often involve economies of scale. For these reasons, some believe that the e-money market will develop similarly to other network industries such as ATMs and credit cards. Initially, there will be a large number of products. However, due to many factors including economies of scale, the number of systems will decrease, resulting in a smaller number of large "branded networks" controlling a majority of the e-money transactions. In these networks, the network and its brand—not the individual issuer would have a strong retail presence and would be the foremost link in the consumer's mind. Although it is impossible to determine whether such a structure will develop in the US, evidence indicates that this may already have occurred for open systems, since there are only a limited number of dominant 'brands' of e-money emerging at this time.

Electronic money and electronic payments systems for retail transactions are commanding widespread attention. These systems, wherein neither legal tender, nor paper checks, nor credit-card numbers change hands at the time of purchase, have already started to spread across the globe. They offer significant and profitable opportunities for changing the way consumers pay for the widest possible range of goods and services. Hardly a month seems to pass without some announcement of another alliance of computer and financial services firms. Organizers' plans invariably envision a broad array of retail financial services and products available in an electronic or digital format.

The electronic transfer of funds is not a new phenomenon in the United States or, indeed, most of the developed world. Large scale and wholesale payment transactions in the United States and other nations have been conducted electronically for some time. What is new today is the expansion of electronic money technology in financial transactions conducted by consumers and smaller, nonfinancial organizations. Electronic wholesale payments in the United States account for a much larger dollar volume of transactions than all retail transactions, but they take place among relatively few parties that have worked long, hard, and successfully at making these transactions secure. Retail transactions, the vast bulk of the number of transactions in the United States, take place among parties who are concerned about both the security and the privacy of those transactions. Developing systems that meet the variety of consumer and merchant needs during a period of evolving technology will be a challenge. Electronic money and the technology that makes it possible raise important questions about the continuing effectiveness of existing government tools and methods used to carry out traditional responsibilities in such areas as consumer protection and law enforcement. Further, in the United States, the operability of much electronic money technology and many electronic money systems for retail payments is largely untested, except in pilot projects and limited experiments.

At the same time, electronic money raises the possibility of actually reducing crime and increasing access for low and moderate income households. It is also quite possible that for competitive reasons private sector purveyors of this new technology will effectively address consumer, criminal, and other issues raised by the development and use of electronic money.

The basis of retail payments evolved gradually from physical coins to paper currency and checks and, more recently and rapidly, from there to debit and credit cards. In large-scale wholesale transactions, money has for decades been transactional information transmitted electronically over closed, wire transfer systems. Now, money in retail transactions is becoming electronic, transformed into information stored on a computer chip in a plastic card or on a personal computer so that it can be transmitted over open information systems, such as the Internet. There are two underlying developments.

Two forces in particular are responsible for pushing advanced economies around the globe into this next phase in the evolution of money. The first is the steep drop in the cost of computing power. The second is the continuing advance in the application of computer technologies to communications systems. Together, these forces are fundamentally changing the character of traditional money and related financial activities and are setting the stage for even greater changes in the years ahead.

The declining price of personal computers over the past decade has been dramatic. Despite reportedly thinning profit margins, that trend continues, while falling prices and enhanced performance also increasingly characterize computer peripherals such as hard drives, modems, and CD ROM drives.

The trend lines for consumer usage of electronic communication innovations are strongly upward. At the end of last year, 8.8 million Americans were connected to their offices by computer, an increase of almost 16 percent over 1994. In the last six years, host computers on the Internet increased by a staggering 4,700 percent. Some analysts have predicted that, by 1997, about six million Americans will be using some form of wireless communication-triple the number for 1995. At the same time, the capacity of communication channels is growing sharply, reducing the time needed to transmit text and graphics.

Those improvements in communication technologies are changing fundamentally the economics of conducting information-related business. As traditional barriers and costs to information-sharing fall, banks and others in the financial information business are better able to achieve economies of scale in storing and moving data. They can more comprehensively assimilate large quantities of financial data on their operations at a lower cost and in less time. They and their customers can have more direct and immediate access to each other, at lower cost. Most strikingly, perhaps, changes in communication and computer technologies also mean that banks and their customers no longer have to conduct their business face-to-face, and, consequently, no longer have to reside in the same country, state, county, or town. As the need for geographic proximity between financial institution and customer fades, so generally does the importance of geography-based procedures, practices, and rules that govern much of the financial services industry today.

New Retail Payments Systems

Advances in computers and communications technology have led to a change of some significance to policy-makers—the development and growth of new retail payments systems. The most noteworthy developments are electronic cash and engaging in financial transactions from home or elsewhere by personal computers.

Electronic Cash

Electronic cash is a claim on a party, most commonly, the issuer, stored in the form of computer code on a card about the size of a credit card or on the hard drive of a computer. Consumers purchase the claim with traditional money. Consumers exchange the claims for goods and services with merchants who are willing to accept the claim as payment. Cards representing such claims often go by the name 'stored value cards' (SVCs).

The technology for storing claims with which to make payments, and other information, on cards ranges from the magnetic strip common to all credit cards to computer chips that store and process information. Cards containing computer chips are called 'smart cards.' One convenient way to understand SVCs is to classify them as representing either 'closed' or 'open' systems. SVCs that are limited to just a few merchants regardless of location or to many merchants in a relatively small geographic area would represent a closed system.

SVCs that consumers could use at many different businesses over a large geographic area would represent an open system. The distinction between closed and open, however, is largely one of degree.

Closed-system SVCs: One example of a closed-system SVC is the system in which the card issuer and the seller of the goods and services are one and the same (the 'merchant-issuer' model). Examples of such cards include: the farecard used by riders of the subway system in Washington, D.C.; cards issued by a number of colleges and universities in the US to students and perhaps employees that holders may use to purchase a variety of goods and services supplied by the college or university; cards issued by public bodies; and cards issued by certain telephone companies to pay for telephone calls.

In these systems, the user buys a claim on the merchant-issuer with traditional money and receives electronic cash in return. When the user buys goods or services from the merchant-issuer, special point of sale (POS) devices record the transactions with the merchant, reducing the value of the electronic cash recorded on the card by the amount of the purchase. Although consumers make purchases in this system with electronic cash, the system is linked to the current payment system by the merchant-issuer's relationship with its bank.

Campus cards, and other such limited distribution cards, are examples of closed-system cards where the issuer and merchant are different parties. One such example is the 1995 Jacksonville Jaguar stadium card. In this case, one bank issued cards that fans could use at the stadium to buy food, drink, and souvenirs at football games. The transactions with these stored value cards work much the same as with the merchant-issuer. The special POS devices record the transaction for the merchant, altering the purchaser's stored value card to reflect the decreased value. The merchant later presents the electronic cash to the bank-issuer by downloading the payment information from the POS, receiving traditional funds in exchange, typically in the form of a deposit balance at the bank. The merchant's bank would then send the electronic cash through the traditional payment system in much the same manner as presenting a check. As with the merchant-issuer systems described above, bank-issued electronic cash in this somewhat more complex 'closed' system would commonly be closely linked to the traditional payments system.

Open-system SVCs: Examples of open-system SVCs exist today in several countries in Europe and the Far East, and to a more limited extent, in the US. They work essentially in the same manner as bank-issued SVCs in closed-systems, with the important exception that a greater variety of businesses over a relatively larger geographic area accept them. Technology, however, can support electronic cash regimes that could operate independently of banks and thus outside traditional payments systems. In these systems, users would buy electronic cash from issuers using traditional money. Users would 'spend' the electronic cash at a merchant, just as in the case of bank-issued electronic cash.

Merchants would then send the electronic cash to the issuer who would redeem it with some form of traditional money such as a check on a bank balance. In this system, the electronic cash would not 'clear' through the traditional payments system, but could circulate outside it. In expansive versions of either bank-issued or nonbank-issued electronic cash, such cash could circulate among users before presentment to merchants, in much the same manner as traditional cash.

Users would have their own special computer equipment enabling them to transfer electronic cash from one user's card to another. Such a transfer often goes by the name 'peer-to-peer' and can be accomplished with some electronic cash systems today. Peer-to-peer transfers of electronic cash would not clear through the traditional payments system, in contrast to peer-to-peer transfers involving paper checks. With such regimes, the only point of contact between the traditional payments system and electronic cash would be the initial purchase of electronic cash from the issuer with the use of traditional money and redemption of electronic cash by merchants.

PC Financial Transactions

The continued development of the personal computer (PC) has given many households the opportunity to conduct financial transactions from their homes, or indeed from any location where they can connect their portable computers to telephone networks. Through the use of special software and a modem, they can connect to the system used by their financial institution to examine accounts, issue orders to transfer funds among their own accounts, issue orders to transfer funds to the accounts of other parties (e.g., to pay bills or send funds to others), and apply for loans. In some cases, households dial a number that connects them directly with their financial institution. In other cases, households connect to their banks by using the Internet.

After gaining access to the World Wide Web portion of the Internet through their Internet service provider, households go to the Web page sponsored by their bank and conduct their business. Currently, most retail electronic banking involves transmission of information over relatively protected telephone networks or limited access networks of computers called intranets. To date, such systems have not given rise to significant security breaches. Even so, the widespread availability of powerful home computers poses the risk of financial crime, creating incentives for maintaining tight controls and security systems. Strong security systems will be especially important for successful banking and commerce over the more open Internet, where packets of information can pass through a number of computers, each one accessible to a large number of people, before reaching their final destination.

PC-based electronic cash: Technology permits the transmission of electronic cash over networks that link personal computers and the storage of electronic cash on the hard drives of personal computers. PC-based electronic cash is thus one means of paying for goods purchased over the Internet. The possible points of contact between PC-based electronic cash and the traditional payment system are functionally identical to those between SVCs and the payment system. So long as merchants regularly redeem such cash for traditional forms of money and there is little, if any, peer-to-peer transfers, PC-based electronic cash will be a simple adjunct to, not separate from the existing payments system. Regimes with peer-to peer transfers and little, if any, redemption of electronic cash for traditional money would offer the possibility of separate payments systems. As in the case of stored value cards, the popularity of such systems remains somewhat unclear for the immediate future.

Understanding the speed with which electronic money develops, and the actual systems that will be marketed and by whom, is key to the formulation of government policy. Notwithstanding a considerable amount of excitement over the development of electronic money in the press, the pace of moving from the analog world of retail payments to the digital world of electronic money is likely to be slower that many may think. Today, electronic banking is just beginning to become popular, electronic commerce and payments over the Internet are in their infancy, and principal use of SVCs in this country is in a relatively few closed systems. Nevertheless, financial and nonfinancial firms are spending billions of dollars to ensure the success of this market, and there is a clear public interest in these new products. As electronic money and banking products mature it may well turn out that many of the policy issues raised by these new technologies—money laundering, counterfeiting, fraud, consumer disclosure, access for low and moderate income households—will be resolved by the private sector. Beyond this, some policy issues—the loss of seignorage and the impact on monetary policy-only become important when there is widespread use of electronic cash.

Innovators will have ample incentive to introduce new products that will help solve many of the potential problems associated with electronic money. Inappropriate government intervention could delay, deny, or limit the quality of such improvements. Government will have to take care not to act in a manner that stifles innovation. At the same time, it is incumbent upon government to follow these developments carefully, in particular monitoring the pace of change, so that where there are emerging issues that can only be dealt with by government, they are in fact addressed. E-money participants may find that some regulation is necessary to assure consumer confidence and an acceptable environment for commerce develop.

Smart-card usage in the United States

Compared with several other countries, the United States has been slower to take up multi-user smart-card activity, although some usage has developed. The stadium card noted earlier is one example and the experiment conducted by VISA International during the 1996 Olympic Games in Atlanta, Georgia is another. The slow adoption of these systems in the United States may be explained by the abundance and convenience of other payment options. Many US consumers have access to cash, credit cards, checks, and debit cards, and for any purchase can select the payment option that best meets their needs. Another contributing factor may be the sheer size of the United States as compared to countries such as Belgium, Denmark, Finland, and Portugal where smart-card usage is more advanced. How long, then, will it take for US consumers to ultimately decide to embrace electronic money to any significant degree? Widespread electronic money use in the United States, particularly over open systems such as the Internet, seems to be at least two years away. The forces for change, however, are strong. There is considerable commercial interest in developing these new means of payment in the United States for both closed and open systems. As says that earlier there are growing applications of electronic cash technology to such arenas as transportation systems, college and university campuses, and even sports complexes.

Several firms such as VISA International, MasterCard, Mondex, and Proton in various alliances with banks are investing large sums of money into projects that will develop into open systems. Such ventures may need more than a few years to prove their merit. If consumer acceptance of electronic money parallels the history of automated teller machines (ATMs), direct deposit, the credit card, and banking by personal computer, growth in electronic money usage will be slow and limited for the first five years, but increasing dramatically thereafter.

Internet Commerce

Although the subject of much discussion, the actual level of Internet commerce remains modest by any standards. Scattered, unofficial estimates, the only ones available, suggest a level in the range of $100 million to $200 million in annual transactions. The growth of Internet commerce may increase the volume of Internet financial transactions, but will not necessarily guarantee the growth of electronic money. Some observers believe that efforts to reduce the cost of credit card transactions will be successful and that credit cards, one of the most ubiquitous substitutes for money payments in the United States, will become the dominant Internet payment vehicle. They cite the existence of a huge, familiar, and successful infrastructure currently supporting credit card purchases and clearings.

Despite the current level of electronic money activity in the United States, the forces stimulating faster growth in electronic money and commerce here are strong, and the pace of change could quicken. These forces include:

— Expanding electronic-based government payments The need for greater efficiency in government operations is perhaps stronger today than ever before. The question here is, 'How should the government use electronic money in its drive for greater efficiency?' Government has already begun to formulate its answer. The Debt Collection Act of 1996 and the electronic benefit transfer (EBT) initiative are but two examples of recent efforts to achieve greater efficiency. The implications of these and related measures on Treasury operations are substantial.

— *Debt Collection Act:* The Debt Collection Act of 1996 mandates government use of electronic funds transfers (EFT) for all government payments, except tax refunds, by 1999. This includes the payment of government benefits. The act has two effective dates. After July 26, 1996, every new recipient of government payments must accept them electronically, unless the recipient certifies that he or she does not have an account at a financial institution. After January 1, 1999, all payments made to individuals and businesses-including those to persons without accounts at a financial institution-must be made electronically. The Financial Management Service (FMS), a U.S. Department of the Treasury bureau, has adopted an interim rule as part of its plan for implementing the new law. The interim rule implements the requirements of the new law that became effective July 26, 1996, and establishes the responsibilities of federal agencies and federal payment recipients. Agency responsibilities. The interim rule requires all federal agencies to make payments electronically to individuals who, on or after July 26, 1996:

— apply for federal benefit payments;

— begin employment with a federal agency;

— apply for retirement benefits;

— enter into a contract or purchase order with the federal government; or

— file or renew a grant application.

Recipient responsibilities: The interim rule requires each recipient of a federal payment to designate a financial institution or authorized payment agent through which a federal payment may be made. If the individual does not have an account with a financial institution or an authorized payment agent, the individual must certify that in writing to the agency. Implementation of the new requirements by those paying and receiving benefits could help provide those without bank accounts better access to mainstream financial services.

EBT programmes: Even before passage of the Debt Collection Improvement Act, the federal government had taken some initial steps toward realizing the efficiencies promised by electronic money. One such step was the formation of a federal task force that would coordinate the development of EBT programs. Such programs substitute for benefit delivery systems used by both federal and state agencies. In one type of EBT program, the value of food stamps to an individual, and codes indicating the acceptable purchases that the individual could make with the electronic funds, would be encoded in the computer chip embedded in a stored value card. Benefit recipients use these cards in lieu coupons or vouchers to pay for goods and services at merchants and others equipped to receive this form of electronic payment.

Impact on Treasury operations: Conversion of Treasury payments, now running at about 800 million a year, to an all electronic format will bring changes permitting, for example, a consolidation of disbursing operations that currently produce checks. With regard to retail payments, the complete displacement of traditional cash is unlikely. About 18 billion in currency notes valued at approximately $400 billion circulate world wide, despite the growth in checks and wire transfers. Demand is especially strong outside the United States where about $270 billion circulates. There, among the less technologically advanced countries, cash is the principal means of payment, the dollar seems to be one of the currencies of choice, and the infrastructure that will support widespread use of electronic money seems many years away.

Impact on electronic money: The US government is the largest receiver and disburser of payments in the world, and as it makes ever increasing use of electronic payments it is likely to have an influence on operating standards for electronic payments systems. That is because it must ensure any system it uses meets its requirements for security, reliability,.and accuracy. To the extent it adopts stored value technology, it will greatly affect interoperability standards. Thus, the pace at which the public sector seeks to implement electronic payments could have a significant effect on private-sector planning and related activity.

Greater efficiencies for businesses

Lower costs: Electronic money eliminates the costs of handling coin and currency. The estimated cash handling cost for US retailers and banks is over $60 billion annually, which includes costs associated with the processing and accounting of money, as well as storage, transport, and security. Electronic money brings greater efficiency to those tasks, offering substantial cost savings.

According to the National Automated Clearing House Association (NACHA), the cost savings to the banking industry alone flowing from the new requirement for federal EFT payments could be sizeable. For example, NACHA: 'Studies have shown that a financial institution saves between $.75 and $1.25 for each payment converted from a deposit made with a teller to Direct Deposit,' and consequently, 'annual costs savings to the banking industry as a result of these new electronic payments should run between $350 million and $500 million.'

Electronic money potentially provides merchants with cost savings resulting from: reduced collection and deposit float associated with coin, currency, and checks, and faster funds availability; increased sales due to faster throughput at checkout counters and consumer tendencies to spend more with stored value cards; and increased self-serve transactions. Acceptance of electronic money would allow merchants to move more commerce from the physical world to the Internet, which offers access to global markets at low cost. The continuing rapid decline in the cost of technology will increase the extent of these cost savings, enhance innovation, and further increase the attraction of electronic money and finance.

Reductions in some forms of fraud: While magnetic strip debit and credit cards can be overwritten or copied, smart cards are fitted with tamper-resistant chips and strong cryptographic protocols. Additionally, smart cards could be tied to biometric identification mechanisms, such as voice, hand, or retinal prints, to verify the identity of the user. To the extent electronic money displaces checks, moreover, check fraud may be reduced. The new systems will be, however, targets of criminal activity.

Greater safety and security: Another benefit electronic money offers merchants is increasing safety and security by eliminating some opportunities for theft. Electronic money could help curtail vandalism of vending machines, public phones, and the like, because there would be no coin or currency to steal. Similarly, owners and employees of retail establishments and other service providers who handle cash, such as taxicab drivers, could be much less vulnerable to robbery.

More value-added services: Electronic money technology-particularly smart card applications-could help sharpen merchants' offers of value-added services, strengthening customer relationships. For example, retailers could track customer activities (to an even greater extent than they currently do with credit cards) to discern buying patterns and offer buyer-specific discounts and loyalty programs. These targeted promotions, also known as 'micro-marketing,' are generally viewed as more efficient than the mass-marketing techniques currently used. Some hard-pressed communities may benefit. If merchants did not need to collect and store cash, they might be willing to locate in areas that they now see as unacceptably risky.

New choices for consumers

One of the biggest advantages of electronic money is that it is more convenient than other payment mechanisms for small-value purchases. It is faster and easier than exchanging cash and making change, writing a check, or getting a credit card authorization. For all micro-payments, including those on the Internet, sending a 10 cent digital coin for a small purchase of information could prove to be more convenient and less costly than using a credit card.

Obstacles to growth

Despite those benefits, uncertainties on the part of consumers and merchants about the underlying technology could slow widespread use and acceptance of electronic money systems. Some of these uncertainties focus on how well the technology secures personal transactions information over the Internet from theft and related forms of abuse such as false or non-authentic commitments. Other uncertainties arise from concerns about whether or not competing forms of electronic-money for use outside the Internet will require idiosyncratic computer hardware and software. Still others arise from the fact that innovation is often fast-paced, creating doubts about how long any particular technology will be at hand.

Internet security and authentication

Security: Many analysts believe that the use of electronic payments on the Internet will depend on the development of widely available systems that guarantee the security of credit card numbers and the various forms of electronic money. There are numerous mathematical formulas to code or encrypt such numbers, as well as electronic cash, in a way that seriously complicates the task of stealing them or interfering with the intended use. Experts tend to evaluate methods of encryption in terms of the difficulty knowledgeable parties would face in decoding or decrypting the information. There can be differences of opinion among experts on the strength of any particular form of encryption and such differences could contribute to consumer, and merchant, unease.

The availability and strength of encryption seems to be on the minds of some consumers: In informal surveys, consumers cite lack of security as the primary reason they are reluctant to purchase goods and services online. At the same time, consumers routinely send credit cards and credit card numbers through the postal system and over the phone to catalog merchants and offer them to anonymous clerks at retail counters. Such different results suggest that security per se may not be crucial to the success of electronic money on the Internet.

Encryption is not the only form of security of concern to consumers: Traditional cash and credit card transactions suggest that some consumers seem to value written verification of the basic facts of a retail transaction-the name of the seller, a description of the goods or services purchased, and the cost. The seller ordinarily offers the buyer a piece of paper containing those details. Consumers may want their use of electronic money, especially electronic cash, to create similar information. How issuers meet that need may determine the pace of electronic money growth.

Authentication: If consumers are to use electronic money over the Internet they must have confidence in the issuers of the electronic money and the merchants who accept it. Consumers may demand that a trusted third party certify or authenticate the legitimacy of both those parties. Confidence is particularly important for the development of Internet commerce with its virtual shopkeepers that consumers cannot see and evaluate in the traditional way.

Confidence is a two-way street: Merchants will want assurances that the consumers from whom they receive orders for goods and services are the consumers who really want them and that verified consumers will not refuse to meet their responsibilities as defined by law. A trustworthy and reliable system of authentication can provide comfort to merchants on both fronts. Merchants could require customers to sign orders with encrypted digital signatures that can be authenticated by trusted and reliable third parties. Such authentication would unambiguously identify the consumer and provide proof that the consumer requested the goods or service. Trustworthy authentication can also boost electronic communication among businesses, ranging from merchandise orders to contracts that bind all manner of business contracts. Authenticated digital signatures could, for example, substitute for the notary public of the analog world.

There is a growing concern among policy makers and consumer groups in Europe and the United States that individual privacy is greatly compromised by electronic commerce and electronic payments. Such concerns are of course not limited to recent developments regarding electronic money or payments, inasmuch as they apply to current use of credit cards. However, electronic money and payments are likely to materially increase the intensity of debate over these issues for several reasons. SVCs raise the possibility of tracking and recording virtually every payment an individual makes. Such extensive tracking and recording raise issues of extensive target-marketing, government surveillance, and even personal safety as patterns of behavior are mined from this potentially rich data.

In addition, the Internet raises serious concerns about the data being examined by unauthorized persons. Balanced against this is the potential for data created and stored in an electronic money environment to aid law enforcement authorities in preventing crimes and tracking criminals (and, indeed, some of the data may be essential for effective law enforcement efforts). As well, legitimate use of such data could help firms to be more efficient in their marketing efforts.

Interoperability: Most observers agree that electronic money will not find widespread use until technical experts solve the problem of interoperability. In the context of electronic money, the term interoperability captures the extent to which debit cards and stored value cards from different issuers use a common set of standards. These standards govern such issues as the size of the cards (length, thickness, and width) the location and size of the magnetic strip or computer chip, and the coding technology manufacturers use to store information on the magnetic strip or computer chip. They also cover other matters such as the design and workings of devices that "read" the cards. The greater the acceptance of common standards, the greater the degree of interoperability.

Large-scale interoperability would help promote acceptance of electronic money: Merchants generally would be more inclined to invest in card readers if one reader could service a variety of debit and stored value cards. Similarly, with large-scale interoperability consumers could be reasonably confident that many merchants would accept many forms of electronic money. In sum, the greater the number of merchants accepting electronic money the greater the inclination among consumers to use it; the greater the number of consumers using electronic money, the greater the number of merchants willing to accept. Interoperability made possible the success of credit cards and ATMs.

Technological change: Another potential problem is technical change itself. The march of technological innovation seems unending, offering opportunities for improving communications and computer capabilities. Such 'progress' can be disconcerting for consumers and merchants. It clouds, rather than clarifies, the future, creating incentives to wait for the next round of improvements, if not for the emergence of a technology that seems to be on its way toward winning widespread acceptance.

There is considerable debate about what role government should play in the transition to a digital world. Some argue that the government should play little, if any role and allow the private sector to resolve most of the issues. Others advise the government to go so far as to set all the standards for issuing and using electronic cash, if not be the exclusive issuer of electronic cash. Still others recommend approaches that fall between those two extremes. A look at the role of government in the analog world is helpful in considering the role of government in the digital world. In the analog world of finance, the private sector, through innovation and adjustments in practices, has solved many concerns government might have raised.

At the same time, both industry and the public have looked to government to set and enforce rules that provide a foundation for, among other things, consumer rights and responsibilities, law enforcement protections against financial crimes, and the conduct of money issuers. Given the increasing globalisation of finance, international agreements also come into play. At the same time, there are important differences between the development of electronic money, banking, and commerce today, and the development of other financial services products in the past that make it a bit less clear what the appropriate response of government should be. As says earlier, there is reason to believe that the private sector will work hard to resolve a number of potential policy issues that may emerge as the development of E-money proceeds, and use of E-money becomes more widespread. Moreover, developments are likely to unfold at a pace that allows careful study of potential issues. Accordingly, government must be careful not to overreact to, or stifle, new innovations that can greatly benefit the consumer and the American economy.

Government should take advantage of marketplace solutions to issues where appropriate. To do this, and at the same time to be in a position to act appropriately, it is important for government to maintain expertise in electronic money and payments developments, and to consider carefully major questions presented by these developments. In some areas, such as the issuance of electronic money, additional federal interpretations, rules or, perhaps, laws may be needed to provide an appropriate legal foundation for electronic money systems. In others, existing requirements are no longer relevant and need to be eliminated.

Consumer Issues

One important area of ambiguity in the law involves the rules (including mandatory disclosures) governing many of the financial transactions that are commonplace between consumers and financial firms. Transactional rules for electronic debit systems are relatively well-established, but those for electronic cash are not. The government must decide whether it is best that electronic cash transactional rules evolve by contract, whether it should apply rules and precedents developed for related areas to electronic cash, or if that is not appropriate, whether to develop new rules. A key consideration should be the ability of consumers and merchants to protect adequately their interests by negotiation.

The issue of protecting consumer interests has four parts: To what extent should consumers be liable for electronic cash that is lost, stolen or compromised by the insolvency of the issuer? How much information should an issuer of electronic money disclose to consumers? Will the privacy of electronic-money users be adequately protected? Should the government take steps to ensure that all consumers, including the poor, gain access to electronic money and banking services? Clearly, one issue common to those four questions is whether a given electronic money system is an electronic debit system that transfers value among deposit accounts or an electronic cash system. Since only chartered depositories can accept deposits, and since those firms are highly regulated, the existing statutory regime presents a ready framework within which to address issues raised by electronic debit systems. Electronic cash systems, however, may present significant challenges to policymakers. While most issuers of electronic cash, in all likelihood, will continue to be subject to some form of regulation, the application of existing laws to E-cash instruments is less clear. For some, the answer to these problems might be to restrict the issuance of electronic money to banks. Such a policy at the very beginnings of electronic money development could place unnecessary barriers in the way of competition and innovation, possibly delaying or denying public benefits.

Liability for losses

Most electronic cash holdings will not be insulated against certain kinds of losses, such as misplacement by the holder, theft, and insolvency of the issuer. Misplacement and theft are risks holders of traditional cash incur, but not loss due to the insolvency of the issuer. Some electronic cash issued by banks may have the protection of FDIC insurance, and some issuers may elect to provide holders with protections against loss and theft. Barring substantive changes in law, some electronic cash issued by nonbanks will not be insured by the government against a loss due to issuer insolvency, although state statutes governing money transmitters may reduce the risk of issuer insolvency. Electronic cash issued by banks, however, won't necessarily offer holders insurance against issuer insolvency, and the absence of such insurance would mark a sharp distinction between insured deposits and bank-issued electronic cash. Consumers may, therefore, be confused by the existence of visually indistinguishable electronic cash systems, and policymakers must decide whether this concern warrants legislative or regulatory action.

Disclosure

Existing federal rules governing transactions and disclosure may not extend to some electronic money activities. While the Electronic Fund Transfer Act and Regulation E, which is issued by the Federal Reserve, will apply to consumer electronic debit transactions, no comprehensive body of transactional rules defines the rights and obligations arising from electronic cash transactions. Similarly, detailed consumer disclosures for EFT transactions apply to debit systems, but not necessarily to electronic cash systems. There is likely to be some pressure from consumer groups and some market participants to extend current law to electronic cash systems, as those systems become more commonplace.

Privacy

Electronic commerce and finance creates new opportunities for unauthorized access to and manipulation of private information. Although the European Parliament has moved to address some of those issues, few federal laws address them. The extension of electronic debit and electronic cash systems to the Internet presents additional risks. Data traveling through the open network of the Internet is more susceptible to interception and can be copied or modified. The extent of the risk to privacy will depend on the design of the systems and the types of information traveling over the Internet. Protecting individual privacy in the digital world will be at least as complex as it is in the analog world. Finding the right balance between governmental needs for information to combat crime and individual needs for anonymity will be challenging. That is not the only hurdle.

Consumer data derived from financial transactions covers a broad spectrum of information, and consumers may be more concerned about the confidentiality of some types of information than others. For example, consumers may object strongly to the public release of data describing their income and net worth, but allow some information describing their spending patterns to be used by direct marketers.

Access

Judging the impact of electronic money on groups of consumers, especially the poor, is difficult. On the one hand, the application of advanced technology to finance and commerce could exacerbate current inequities in the access to financial services. The poor are much less able than others to afford computers or to have access to educational opportunities facilitating computer use. As the cost of computers and associated technologies continues to fall, the availability of financial services from traditional outlets such as branches, and perhaps even ATMs, will decline. That trend could also disadvantage those in rural areas where the infrastructure necessary for electronic money and banking is not now in place. On the other hand, not all PC developments need to disadvantage the poor. PC-based systems for banking services offer the potential for a community group or church to work as partners with a bank or other financial-services firm for the delivery of financial services at convenient and safe locations.

Additionally, the technological revolution holds the potential to enhance greatly the ability of the poor to have convenient access to financial services because of the advantages that are inherent to high-tech payments systems. The cost of low-value transactions-transactions most common to the poor-can be much lower in high-tech systems than in traditional payments systems centered, for example, on brick-and-mortar branches. High-tech systems have more flexibility than traditional systems in the delivery of financial services virtually. Evidence of this flexibility is available today in the form of electronic benefit transfer (EBT) systems, banking over the telephone, and to some degree in high-tech branches in supermarkets and convenience stores. Such flexibility provides added convenience, in that services can be available on virtually a 24-hour basis, and added safety, in that funds are less subject to theft. In the not-to-distant future, additional evidence may include the use of home television sets hooked up to cable systems that give access to banking and other services.

Law enforcement

Electronic cash could, depending on how it is developed, share an important attribute with traditional cash. Like cash, it could lead to anonymous transactions that do not leave a 'paper trail.' While those attributes give ordinary citizens privacy, they also make possible the commission of large-scale financial crimes with relatively low risk of apprehension. Should the use of electronic cash become pervasive, government may question the effectiveness of its regulatory provisions and investigative strategies and techniques in combating financial crimes.

Evaluations of those issues will necessarily depend on the particulars of electronic money and electronic cash product. For example, many smart-card systems abroad generate audit trails and limit the maximum 'value' that a card may hold at any time. Countries with such cards suggest that criminal interest in the cards is low. For the most part, the crimes in a world of electronic cash and digital commerce will be familiar: theft, fraud, counterfeiting, tax evasion, and money laundering. To ensure that law enforcement agencies have the necessary tools to combat financial crimes, government will have to determine the impact of electronic money systems on regulations and policies designed to control financial crime, and investigative strategies and techniques. Traditionally, law-enforcement agencies have relied on rules and regulations allowing them to see documents, hear information exchanges, and track or interdict goods in clearly defined jurisdictions in their fight against financial crimes. Such tangible evidence and the certainty of geography will erode in the digital world of electronic money.

Certain laws, such as the Bank Secrecy Act (BSA) and its implementing regulations, require consumers and businesses to provide information that enables the government to combat certain financial crimes. How such laws apply to new electronic payment systems is not clear. Historically, law enforcement and regulatory officials have relied upon banks and other types of financial institutions to provide data 'chokepoints' through which funds from criminal activities must pass.

The BSA, by requiring these institutions to keep records and file, on certain types of financial transactions provides a paper trail that enables law-enforcement officials to deter, detect, investigate, and prosecute illicit activity. Electronic money systems that allow large, unaccountable transactions have the potential, however, to undermine the effectiveness of the BSA. If such electronic money systems are not covered by BSA requirements, there is reasonable certainty that criminals will use them to evade the BSA 'chokepoints.' Electronic cash could lend itself to totally anonymous transactions without a paper trail, increasing the investigative hurdles faced by law-enforcement officials. The application of the BSA requirements to electronic money systems will depend upon whether the participants and products involved in those systems fall within certain definitions of the BSA.

Regulatory policy

Law enforcement and regulatory officials have mechanisms in place for tracking the flow of money derived from illegal activities based on laws and regulations applied to the financial system. With an open system such as the Internet or with electronic 'peer-to-peer' transactions, however, exchanges of financial value may occur that are not technically subject to the BSA. As electronic systems develop and government gains a greater understanding of the transactions conducted over these systems, government must identify what additional regulatory measures, if any, law-enforcement officials need to combat financial crimes.

Investigative techniques

With the advent of home banking and the development of new retail electronic payments systems, there will be fewer and fewer face-to-face financial transactions. Law enforcement agencies are particularly concerned about the ability of financial institutions to 'know their customers' in a potentially anonymous payment system. Further, government is concerned that paperless payment systems with anonymous users will present fewer opportunities to use traditional techniques such as analyses of financial documents, and surveillance of those suspected of financial crimes.

Decryption

Decryption is the reverse process of encryption. It refers to the decoding of messages that the sender altered-encrypted-in an attempt to keep the message secret from all parties except the one who was to receive it. There are many different encryption techniques, but they all revolve around a process of substituting a number, letter, or some other symbol for the true letter or number or symbol. Each process has its own rule for substituting a false symbol for the true one. Sometimes observers call this rule a 'key,' since knowledge of the rule or key will enable an interested party to 'unlock' or decode the encrypted message. Encryption provides the potential for security in the digital world, and in the minds of those with large financial stakes in the development of electronic commerce and money 'security is to the Internet what safety is to the airlines.' Within the last several years, the private sector has made significant strides in strengthening the commercially applicable encryption processes. These advances respond to consumer and business concerns about the authenticity, reliability, and security of buyers and sellers and of purchases and payments, whether transactions are conducted over the Internet or in the shop of a retail merchant. For the private sector, the stronger the encryption, the smaller the cause for concern.

Because of its law-enforcement responsibilities, government has as strong interest in its ability to decrypt encrypted messages and in the advances in encryption technologies. For the government, powerful, private-sector encryption technology can pose challenging issues. Undecipherable encryption could facilitate criminal activities and, potentially, expose the United States to national security risks. To manage those risks, the Administration has proposed development of a Key Management Infrastructure (KMI) that would, with court permission, give selected federal officials access to the "keys" that would unlock messages encrypted using private-sector technology. The debate on the advantages and disadvantages of this proposal is continuing.

Issuers of electronic money

Electronic money cuts across a wide spectrum of interest. Answers to the question have the potential to affect such activities as the regulation and supervision of issuers; and the management of both the payments system and monetary policy. For that reason they deserve discussion. By any measure, electronic money plays a minor role in the US economy and, as noted elsewhere, that role is not likely to increase any time soon. According to some estimates, "80 percent of all retail purchases in the United

States are settled in cash, the vast majority of them for less than $20." Debit cards, the biggest form of electronic money, accounts for about two percent of retail transactions, and credit cards, the most popular electronic payment option, accounts for only 5 percent.

If the government should find that the issuance of electronic cash involves the receipt of 'deposits,' federal laws precluding or restricting deposit-taking by nonbanks might be applied to nonbanks issuing electronic cash. The states could also limit the types of firms that can offer electronic money services.

In Europe, government officials favor banks as issuers of electronic money, reflecting, in part, the availability of a well-structured regulatory regime. In this country, there is a belief among a number of policy makers and knowledgeable private-sector parties that limiting the issuance of electronic cash to banks could stifle competition an innovation. Many also believe that appropriate regulation of the nonbank issuers can effectively resolve the problems they may pose. Designing the appropriate response will be a challenge. Some of the nondepositories may be affiliated with depositories and others may not be affiliated. Subjecting all nonbank electronic money issuers to the full panoply of depository regulation may not be appropriate. Although some requirements may well be appropriate, nonbank issuers, be they affiliated with depositories or not, may not warrant the same regulations regarding capital, asset diversification, and asset quality, for example, that now apply to depositories.

If and when the time for government action arrives, attention should focus on determining how different regulatory structures for depositories and nonaffiliated nondepositories will affect the competition between those two groups, including how consumers may value the regulatory structures. For example, depending upon whether electronic cash is found to be a 'deposit' under certain Federal Reserve rules, banks may incur costs of deposit reserve requirements that are not imposed on nonbank issuers. The government will also need to decide whether providing holders of electronic cash issued by both depositories and nondepositories with the kinds of protection available, for example, from the FDIC would be appropriate.

Payments system stability: Significant electronic money issuance, especially by those outside the traditional banking system, could also pose challenging problems. The operational failure or insolvency of a key issuer could create a widespread loss of confidence in other forms of electronic money, leading, perhaps, to additional insolvencies and a flight to legal tender. Conceivably, the orderly flow of the inter-bank clearing system could be at risk, to the extent that the ability of banks to meet their inter-bank payments depended upon the ability of electronic money issuers to redeem their obligations in traditional bank deposits. This would be of great concern to the Federal Reserve.

Monetary management: Electronic money, if successful, could gradually lead to shifts among different forms of money held by consumers, and thus potentially affect the behavior of the monetary aggregates. However, electronic money may be only one of a number of changes in financial markets in the years ahead. Some of these may require modifications in the details of how monetary policy is implemented, just as other financial innovations have required adjustments in the past. The Federal Reserve believes that it has the capability to adjust to these changing circumstances while continuing to meet its traditional responsibilities. In order to monitor the monetary aggregates, however, the Federal Reserve may need to obtain data on outstanding amounts of electronic money from issuers, similar to the situation with nonbank-issued travelers checks.

The government, as the exclusive issuer of currency, stands to lose revenue if privately issued electronic money significantly displaces the use of legal tender. Legal tender provides revenues in two ways.

— Signorage, the difference between the face value of coins and the cost of making them.

— Government interest payments are reduced to the extent that people hold currency instead of interest-bearing debt.

Some estimates suggest that the reduction in interest payments could be as much as $3.5 billion annually. As noted in the discussion of electronic money and Treasury operations, the likelihood that the adoption of E-money will lead to a significant reduction in avoided interest expenses for the Treasury is small.

International Cooperation

Electronic money systems operating over open systems such as the Internet can, for all intents and purposes, operate outside of clear geographic boundaries. Within the United States, this creates potential questions concerning the applicability of state laws to transactions that may be initiated by a consumer in one state who uses a financial institution headquartered in a second state to make payments to recipients located in still other states, by means of a computer at some unknown location. Those challenges are even greater at the international level. Nation states may find unilateral enforcement of electronic money related rules difficult. Laws such as those involving protection of personal privacy and entities permitted to issue electronic money may raise especially difficult problems, as will those dealing with tax collections. Sales over the Internet, for example, raise questions about the location of a transaction and consequently about which tax laws apply.

Because most electronic payments systems can operate internationally and in multiple currencies, resolving jurisdictional issues for financial crimes will be difficult. This erosion of national boundaries by retail electronic money and payments makes it even more critical for law enforcement and supervisory authorities in different countries to cooperate in their anti-crime activities and to adopt consistently strong law enforcement policies and standards.

Currently, the Financial Action Task Force (FATF), an international enforcement group with representatives from 26 countries, coordinates approaches to financial crimes and related areas. Recently, FATF adopted several recommendations for strengthening the ability of member countries to manage their crime-fighting efforts.

Electronic-money technology can generate and capture a great deal of payments information. This information has substantial value for both commercial and anti-crime purposes. Using such information for those purposes, however, can raise serious questions involving personal privacy. Recently, the European Union (EU) adopted a policy on personal privacy that provides protections that some believe may not be available in US law. Although the guidelines are extensive, they generally try to ensure that data on individuals are: collected for lawful purposes as specified in the directive and processed fairly and lawfully for purposes specified in the directive. Individuals have the right to see the data that pertain to them. The directive also requires those who hold and process personal information to notify individuals of releases of their personal data and, under certain circumstances, to obtain their consent for such release.

Electronic money systems are still in the relatively early stages of development, and the timing of many future developments is likely to be slower than some people expect, for there are many obstacles to growth. These include issues relating to interoperability, security and privacy, and transaction verification and authentication. The prospect of measured growth does not mean that government can simply sit back and wait for problems to develop. This is an area where major developments are taking place that could greatly alter the payments systems domestically and internationally. Policy makers will likely wrestle, sooner rather than later, with questions in four areas:

- Consumer issues-clarifying rights and responsibilities;
- Law enforcement-evaluating the effectiveness of traditional tools in combating financial crimes;
- Government payments-moving steadily toward the complete use of EFT technology; and
- International coordination-reinforcing the foundations of cooperative action across a wide range of issues.

Traditional government responsibility for areas such as payments system stability and monetary policy may require government action, if and when electronic money systems are more fully developed and commonplace, although the timing for that is likely to be well down the road. In acting upon the nearer-term issues, government can have an effect upon the removal of barriers to growth, a process in which the private sector has a considerable financial interest. Electronic payments and EBT initiatives can affect standards for interoperability. Law enforcement needs for information can affect privacy interests of consumers and merchants, as well as the technical standards that provide the security, transaction verification, and authentication of computerized messages. Specification of consumer rights and responsibilities can affect consumer confidence and acceptance of electronic money products.

Consequently, in meeting its responsibilities, government must combine patience with aggressive fact-finding, study, and coordination among government units both nationally and internationally. Premature action among government agencies or decisions based upon incomplete analysis could thwart innovation and its ensuing benefits, including, perhaps, the ability of US firms to compete effectively in global markets. For electronic money and banking, progress is best achieved through innovation by industry, and by government acting when markets are clearly unable to address concerns on their own.

5

Protection of Privacy in Electronic Era

Consumers are becoming increasingly concerned about how personally identifiable information is being used. This concern, if unaddressed, could have the potential to act as an impediment to widespread consumer acceptance of e-money. A significant barrier to the widespread usage of e-money will be lack of consumer trust or confidence in the privacy of the new payment systems. Both fair information practices and anonymous payments will help build that trust. The belief that systems should be developed to ensure consumer privacy and security, rather than having to add privacy protections later in response to demonstrated problems. Several openions are appropriate role for government is to set basic privacy principles to guide businesses as they build consumer privacy and security into their systems. The increase in data collection efficiency associated with e-money could provide merchants and other system participants with an increased ability to obtain personally identifiable consumer information.

Similarly, the diversity, quality, and quantity of information that is collected and the fact that there are multiple places it can be captured and stored, increase the privacy concerns that could arise with electronic money. The trend toward electronic money may eventually reduce a consumer's ability to use cash or other anonymous payment methods, whereas believed that the new technology could promote anonymous payment methods.

Similarly, several industry the use of encryption can enhance the technical security of products and provide greater privacy protection for consumers. The number of parties involved in new payment methods, including issuers, distributors and processors, could result in more people having access to consumer information. The potential for privacy invasions may be greater as cards become multifunctional because more information could be collected and stored in one place.

The consumers may not receive adequate disclosure of what personal data is being collected, who will receive that data, and how the data will be used. The information consumers voluntarily reveal to the issuer and information about their transactions with merchants would be transferred to the issuer's affiliates and to other parties. The self-regulatory actions, such as industry guidelines and privacy policies, do not provide any meaningful protections for consumers because they are largely unenforceable. Additionally, were concerned that the personal information collected through these new electronic payment methods may not be secure from illegal or unauthorized access and use.

The most consumers do not understand and will not be informed of the privacy implications of choosing different payment methods. There must be significant efforts to educate the public about information security and to seek fair information practices.

The governments should work with consumer organizations to help educate consumers about privacy considerations related to e-money. The governments should establish model disclosures and vocabulary to help consumers understand these products. The e-money would give governments greater access to consumers' financial information by eliminating their ability to make payments anonymously. The consumers may believe that auditable e-money systems will increase the government's ability to gain access to financial information. The belief that it is premature to prescribe a particular form of consumer disclosure about privacy, particularly when stored value products are in such an early stage of development and implementation.

The statutory and common law restricts third party access to many types of information. Some say that they currently provide consumers with general information about what information is being collected and the use of that information. Representatives of law enforcement expressed concerns that some of the new payment methods will diminish the government's ability to identify participants in financial transactions.

The use of encryption in e-money systems might make it more difficult for law enforcement authorities to identify, apprehend, and prosecute criminals who use encryption systems to facilitate money-laundering and counterfeiting. The existing constitutional and statutory provisions place many restrictions on governmental access to confidential information. The requiring that e-money issuers maintain detailed transaction records to facilitate law enforcement could chill product innovation and increase issuer costs, possibly hindering market acceptance of new payment products.

Privacy Issues

Consumer concerns about the privacy of their financial information extend beyond privacy in e-money transactions, and are varied and complex. Some consumers are extremely protective of their privacy and view any collection or use of personally identifiable information as an intrusion, while others are far less concerned about privacy-related matters. Although consumers' privacy thresholds are not uniform, consumers generally share certain key privacy concerns. First, consumers want to receive adequate information about an entity's information collection and use policies. Consumers also appear to be concerned about secondary use of information—the use of information for purposes other than the original transaction, either by the information collector or by a third-party to whom the information is sold or transferred (e.g., a third party processor). The potential for privacy intrusions seems to be at its greatest in these cases, where consumers may not be aware that their personal information is being put to new uses or have any control over those uses. Obtaining knowledge of an issuer's information use policies would allow consumers choice, i.e., so that they can make an informed decision about what e-money product is appropriate for their privacy needs. Additionally, disclosures could provide consumers with rights of redress should the issuer misuse their personal information in a way that is inconsistent with the disclosures or violated public policy.

Existing laws may limit access to, and use of, consumers' e-money information by issuers and third parties. However, unlike the nations of Western Europe, the United States does not have universal or omnibus privacy laws. A consumer's right to financial privacy has not been established as a fundamental right by the United States Supreme Court. Privacy protections in 80 the United States, have evolved on a sectoral basis (applying to certain sectors of society, e.g., banking industry or the public sector), reflecting in part how federal and state legislatures address competing policy objectives, including the prevention and prosecution of criminal acts. There are several existing privacy laws that may or may not apply to e-money.

Many openions expressed concern that consumers would not receive adequate information about an issuer's information practices. Some issuers will provide these disclosures, in an effort to distinguish their products from those of their competitors; however, market incentives may be insufficient to ensure that all consumers receive disclosures about an issuer's information policies. Moreover, existing legal requirements for disclosure of information policies may be inapplicable to most forms of e-money presently in the marketplace.

The Electronic Fund Transfer Act ('EFTA') and its implementing regulation, the Federal Reserve Board's Regulation E, establish the rights and liabilities of consumers who maintain an account at a financial institution and use electronic funds transfers ('EFTs') into or out of the account. Among other things, Regulation E requires financial institutions to document EFTs in writing and to disclose certain information to their customers. Among the disclosures financial institutions must provide to consumers is a description of the circumstances in the institution's 'ordinary course of business' in which it will disclose information about the consumer's account to third parties.

The FCRA enumerates the permissible purposes for obtaining a consumer programmes, including: where the consumer has given his or her written permission; in connection with a credit transaction or insurance underwriting; for employment purposes; and, if there is a legitimate business need, in connection with a business transaction initiated by the consumer. Information solely about transactions or experiences between a consumer and an entity, however, may be shared generally by the entity. Recent amendments to the FCRA expand the scope of permissible information-sharing among affiliates. Affiliated persons and entities are now permitted to share and use consumer information—including consumer programmes among themselves without becoming consumer programming agencies subject to the FCRA, provided the consumer receives notice and an opportunity before the consumer's information is shared to direct that the information not be shared ("opt-out").

Businesses may communicate their own transactional information about a consumer to a consumer reporting agency without notice to the consumer. To ensure the accuracy of this information, however, the FCRA amendments require that persons who furnish information to a consumer reporting agency avoid furnishing knowingly inaccurate information, correct and update information reported, and notify the consumer programming agency of disputes and account closures. It is uncertain whether consumer's e-money transaction information would fall under the protection of the FCRA for several reasons:

— e-money issuers may not be considered "consumer reporting agencies."

— the data collected-information on the consumer's spending patterns-may not fall within the definition of a "consumer report," for example, if the information is considered to be experience information.

However, e-money issuers that provided information to a consumer agency would be subject to the requirements of the FCRA regarding furnishers.

Several federal statutes may limit the government's access to consumers' e-money information. The Privacy Act of 1974 ('Privacy Act') controls the federal government's collection, use, and disclosure of information on individuals. It does not apply to state government agencies or the private sector. A federal agency may collect only such information about an individual as is relevant and necessary to accomplish a required agency function and the agency must provide a Privacy Act statement to each individual asked to supply information. The Privacy Act prohibits, with limited exceptions, a federal agency from disclosing any such record to any person or to another agency unless the individual to whom the record pertains has either requested the disclosure or consented to it in writing.

The Right to Financial Privacy Act ('RFPA') prohibits the federal government from accessing or obtaining information in a customer's financial records from a financial institution, and prohibits a financial institution from disclosing such information to the federal government, except pursuant to the customer's authorization, an administrative subpoena or summons, a search warrant, a judicial subpoena, or a formal written request. The RFPA defines a 'financial institution' as any office of a bank, savings bank, credit card issuer, industrial loan company, trust company, savings association, building and loan, homestead association, credit union, or consumer finance institution. The RFPA only covers 'financial records,' defined to include 'information known to have been derived from' a record pertaining to a customer's relationship with a financial institution. It is uncertain whether the RFPA would apply to a consumer's e-money transaction information for several reasons:

— the scope of institutions subject to the RFPA is limited, although many current e-money issuers would most likely fall within the RFPA's definition of 'financial institutions.'

— a consumer's e-money transaction information may not, in all instances, be considered to be a [financial record' relating to an 'account' for purposes of the RFPA.

Although the US has various sectoral privacy laws protecting some consumer financial information, it is uncertain whether these protections would extend to e-money. Accordingly, existing laws may not address consumer concerns about the collection and use of their e-money information, require issuers to disclose how information will be collected and used, provide consumers with the ability to control whether unaffiliated third parties can obtain the information, or generally limit government access to the information.

In US the Federal laws prohibiting unauthorized access to electronic communications may be applicable to the security of e-money payment information. The Electronic Communications Privacy Act ('ECPA') prohibits the unauthorized access or use of any facility through which an electronic communication service is provided or to intentionally exceed the authorization for accessing that facility. 'Electronic communications' is defined broadly and includes any transfer of signs, signals, writing, images, sounds, or intelligence of any nature transmitted by a wire, or electromagnetic or photo-electronic system, except electronic funds transfer information stored by a financial institution.

The ECPA also prohibits any person or entity from knowingly divulging to any person or entity the contents of an electronic communication while that communication is in transmission or in electronic storage. Again, it is unclear whether a consumer's e-money transaction information would fall within the ECPA's prohibition against disclosing electronic communications in transmission or storage.

Information on consumers and their preferences has important economic value to businesses and consumers. It can help businesses better allocate their resources, improve product quality, and assist consumers in product and service choice. Information can aid firms in the design and delivery of products and services, in marketing, and in inventory control. Although some information, such as mailing lists or product purchase patterns, has always been used for marketing purposes, technological advances of recent years have made that information easier to develop and cheaper to replicate.

Consequently, firms are able to make better use of existing information and to lower the costs of developing new information sources. Information resources can also generate their own independent source of revenue when replicated, sorted, and sold. In some cases, the revenue from direct sale of information might make the provision of primary services profitable. The development and use of consumers' information, however, also raises important questions about consumers' privacy.

The heightened public debate in recent years about privacy and electronic technology has begun to make financial industry participants more sensitive to issues surrounding the collection and dissemination of customer information. As in the financial services sector more generally, industry responses that could be relevant to e-money are continuing to evolve. For example, many products can be purchased on an anonymous basis, such as through vending machines. Similarly, the development of more anonymous e-money products is, itself, one market response that has the potential to provide consumers with new ways to enhance their privacy in financial transactions.

Industry responses based on new, more anonymous technologies may be constrained, however, by law enforcement concerns, which may constitute a significant barrier to the development of electronic money products with greater protections. Although it is too early to tell how many e-money products will ultimately develop, it is likely that more anonymous products will emerge if there is consumer demand for the products and law enforcement concerns can be accommodated. For example, consumer preferences might emerge for anonymous small dollar payments, which would not infringe on the important interests of government agencies to review suspicious large dollar transactions.

Current e-money technology is capable of delivering products with varying effects on privacy, ranging from fully anonymous, cash-like systems, in which no personally identifiable transaction records are created, to fully auditable systems that can identify and store every transaction conducted by every consumer.

As the technology evolves, new products will be developed. The extent to which new products will incorporate privacy protections will be influenced by several factors, including consumer preferences, law enforcement needs, and industry perceptions of the value of information. Consumers with a high degree of concern about the privacy of their transactions will likely favor cash or other cash-like payment products that preserve their anonymity. Other consumers are willing to surrender a degree of privacy in their consumer transactions in order to obtain consumer benefits available with auditable systems, such as convenience, error resolution, recovery of value for lost cards, purchase protection, and loyalty program awards. The majority of stored value systems in existence today involve some trade-off between these types of consumer benefits and privacy. Some e-money issuers claim that it is possible to combine some consumer benefits of an auditable system with the anonymity of a cash-like system, decreasing the need for this trade-off.

At the present time, whether consumers will demand e-money products that protect their privacy is uncertain. How widespread the existence of privacy protections will become may depend on the extent to which consumers tend to prefer products that offer these protections. Given the strong competing pressures from cash and other payment methods, issuers are more likely to face pressures to provide privacy protections, especially as consumer awareness over information collection and use rises and consumers increasingly seek such protections. Issuers in such an environment might see offering privacy protection as a way to differentiate their product, competing for customers on the basis of the privacy protections offered. Similarly, some issuers may then create a product for which consumers would, in effect, pay a premium in exchange for additional privacy protections. While there is reliable evidence that consumers are reluctant to commit to electronic commerce and e-money because of privacy concerns, a clear market demand for this 'privacy premium' product has yet to emerge.

Consumers that are not particularly concerned about the confidentiality of their purchases may not demand privacy protections or information about disclosure policies, as is currently the case for credit cards and similar payment vehicles. Market developments may in some respects address consumer concerns about privacy. Moreover, even if individual consumers do not demand specific protections—due to lack of knowledge or otherwise—implementation of privacy protections by individual firms could increase consumer confidence overall and thereby foster development of the e-money market. In addition, many financial industry participants, either individually or as part of industry groups, are exploring self-regulatory responses to consumer privacy concerns in the financial services industry more generally. Several groups have voluntarily established privacy policies or codes of fair information practices. Also, several industry groups are considering developing 'Acceptance' or 'Privacy' marks.

The SmartCard Forum's Privacy Guidelines encourage their members to: respect the privacy expectations of consumers; ensure that the data are as current, accurate, and complete as possible; promptly honor consumers' requests for information that a company has about them; enable consumers to correct inaccurate personally identifiable information; limit the use, collection, and retention of customer information; and apply appropriate security measures to protect consumer data. The SmartCard Forum principles also encourage their members to provide consumers the opportunity to opt-out before personally identifiable consumer information is to be provided to unaffiliated third parties for marketing or similar purposes. Third parties receiving the information from SmartCard members are encouraged to adhere to equivalent privacy standards with respect to that information.

Similarly, the guidelines suggest that service providers should implement policies and procedures to limit employee access to personally identifiable consumer information on a need-to-know basis, educate employees about the privacy guidelines and their responsibilities under the guidelines, and monitor employee compliance, taking appropriate disciplinary action where appropriate. In September 1997, the American Bankers Association ('ABA'), The Bankers Roundtable and its division, the Bank Information Technology Secretariat ('BITS'), the Consumer Bankers Association (CBA), and the Independent Bankers Association of America ('IBAA'), endorsed a common set of privacy principles ('Banking Industry Principles'). These principles provide that subscribing financial institutions should:

- recognize a consumer's expectation of privacy by making available privacy guidelines and/or providing a series of questions and answers about financial privacy to their customers;
- only collect, retain and use individual customer information where it would be useful (and allowed

by law) to administer that organization's business and to provide products, services, and other opportunities to its customers;

— establish procedures to ensure customer information is accurate, current, and complete in accordance with reasonable commercial standards, including responding to requests to correct inaccuracies in a timely manner;

— limit employee access to personally identifiable information to those with a business reason for knowing such information, educate employees so that they will understand the importance of confidentiality and customer privacy, and take appropriate disciplinary measures to enforce employee privacy responsibilities;

— maintain appropriate security standards and procedures regarding unauthorized access to customer information;

— not reveal specific information about customer accounts or other personally identifiable information to unaffiliated third parties for their independent use, except for the exchange of information with reputable information reporting agencies to maximize the accuracy and security of such information or in the performance of bona fide corporate due diligence, unless 1) the information is provided to help complete a customer-initiated transaction, 2) the customer requests it, 3) the disclosure is required by/ or allowed by law or 4) the customer has been informed about the possibility of such disclosure for marketing or similar purposes through a prior communication and is given the opportunity to decline;

— if personally identifiable information is given to a third party, the financial institution should insist that the third party adhere to similar privacy principles that provide for keeping such information confidential;

— devise methods of providing a customer with an understanding of their privacy principles. In conjunction with the privacy principles, BITS is in the process of developing a plan for implementing the principles. Thus far, the BITS Board of Directors, made up of the Chairs of the largest banks in the United States, as well as representatives of the ABA, IBAA, and Bankers Roundtable, have approved and endorsed the 'Privacy Principles Implementation Plan.' This plan states that: a plan for implementing the privacy principles will be approved at the level of the Board of Directors or the Office of the Chair of the bank; bank policies related to customer privacy will be communicated to bank customers; employees will be informed and educated about the bank's plan to implement the privacy principles; banks will obtain agreements from third-party vendors on a case-by-case basis to comply with the bank's privacy principles; where a bank provides information to unaffiliated third parties for their independent use for marketing or similar purposes, the bank will notify customers of their right to opt-out from the information sharing; banks will establish and maintain procedures by which customers can correct inaccurate information, and banks will establish internal policies to ensure compliance with and to address breaches of a bank's privacy policy. These principles are more likely to address consumers' privacy concerns in a meaningful and effective manner if they involve a means to assure adherence by industry participants.

Certain industry self-regulatory initiatives include a compliance assurance mechanism. For example, the members of the Individual Reference Services Group ('IRSG') have agreed to self-regulatory principles that require an annual review by a 'reasonably qualified independent professional service' to assess whether the reference service is in compliance with the IRSG's principles. The results of this review must be made public. Also signatories to the principles have agreed only to sell information to reference service companies in compliance with the principles. Separately, a company's failure to honor its own stated privacy policy may also constitute a deceptive practice prohibited by the Federal Trade Commission Act ('FTCA') and state law.

The Federal Trade Commission Act prohibits any person or corporation from engaging in unfair and deceptive acts or practices in or affecting commerce. Even if any industry self-regulatory policies are not implemented through a formal mechanism for enforcement, the interplay of these practices with existing law may result in certain remedies being available to consumers.

— A court may find that the consumer's reliance on an issuer's stated privacy policy gave rise to a contractual relationship between the consumer and the issuer concerning the terms of the privacy policy. Thus, the issuer's failure to follow the terms of the policy statement could constitute a breach of contract.

— A consumer may argue that the issuer's failure to follow its privacy statement was a breach of warranty.

— Consumers may have actions in tort for negligent misrepresentation.

Both the SmartCard Forum guidelines and the Banking Industry Principles appear to generally address many consumer privacy concerns. Each set of guidelines appears to encourage practices that address certain concerns about the collection and use of information. However, neither set has yet developed a formal means to assure adherence by participants or other members of industry. The lack of a means to assure adherence may limit the effectiveness of these guidelines.

The consumers were concerned that e-money technology would enable issuers and merchants to obtain large amounts of information about them. Similarly, the consumers were concerned that they would not receive adequate disclosure about an issuer's information practices, and that issuers would be able to share a consumer's e-money transaction information with third parties without the consumer's consent. The increased efficiency of data collection methods associated with e-money may increase the potential for privacy intrusions.

The technology provides opportunities for increased privacy, and that different privacy policies and product characteristics may be appropriate for different consumers depending on their disparate individual preferences relating to privacy. Moreover, e-money is in an early stage of development, and there is not yet any indication that anonymous payment methods will not remain available. Additionally, existing laws and market responses may address some consumer concerns. Industry participants appear to have significant incentives to develop an e-money market for consumers especially concerned about privacy.

Privacy protections are essentially evolutionary in the United States, and there is little precedent for comprehensive government established privacy protections. Until e-money has had more time to develop, it is premature to assess whether and the degree to which it will present threats to privacy that would warrant government action. As the e-money industry changes and matures, the extent to which industry participants have effectively addressed consumer privacy interests through self-regulatory initiatives should be carefully monitored. The need for government action regarding privacy standards for e-money then can be reassessed based on the growth of e-money as a payment media and the success of e-money providers in implementing effective privacy principles and policies.

Privact Compliance and Enforcement Mechanisms

Privacy compliance and enforcement are different topics, but are interrelated. They are different, since compliance refers to the level of adherence to legal requirements, while enforcement refers to the mechanisms which can be used to compel such adherence and to protect the rights of data subjects when violations occur. At the same time, the two are closely interrelated, since the higher the level of compliance, the less need there is for enforcement, and a strong level of enforcement may motivate actors to adopt a higher level of compliance. This matter recognises the close interrelationship between these two topics, and thus deals with compliance and enforcement together, while still recognising the potential distinctions between them.

On March 12, 2002, a Questionnaire on Compliance with and Enforcement of Privacy Protection in the

Context of Business-to-Consumer Electronic Commerce was sent to OECD governments and private sector participants. It was developed as part of the work programme of the ICCP Working Party on Information Security and Privacy (WPISP) to fulfil the objectives of the OECD Ministerial Declaration on the Protection of Privacy on Global Networks issued at the OECD Ministerial Conference in Ottawa, Canada in October 1998. Responses were received from 20 member countries and three private organisations. In the Declaration, Ministers declared that they will take steps to ensure that effective enforcement mechanisms are available both to address non-compliance with privacy principles and policies and to ensure access to redress. Moreover, the Declaration calls on the OECD 'to promote user education and awareness about online privacy issues and the means at their disposal for protecting privacy on global networks.'

Compliance and enforcement have become central issues in privacy protection since the OECD Ministerial Conference was held. Considering the limitations of purely legalistic and regulatory approaches, both governments and the private sector have been developing alternative methods of compliance and enforcement which make use of self-regulation, market incentives, technological means, and other mechanisms which go beyond traditional regulatory approaches, and which can better cope with the borderless and fast-moving nature of electronic commerce. It was thus the appropriate time to take stock of compliance and enforcement mechanisms used in the OECD member countries and analyse whether they cope adequately with the requirements of electronic commerce. Respondents were requested to provide basic information rather than detailed analysis. Governments were requested to answer the questions with regard to any 'legal provisions', meaning any domestic laws or regulations, including court decisions (case law), or conventions, treaties or other international legal instruments.

Information was solicited both about governmental agencies (such as a government ministry) and independent privacy regulators (such as a data protection authority), the term 'government agency' refers to both types of entities. Input was also solicited from the private sector, since the private sector can provide practical experience, highlighting the process it undertakes when implementing privacy safeguards. Thus, private sector participants were requested, in addition to providing information on legal provisions they are familiar with as described above, also to provide information on any self-regulatory solutions which they are aware of, such as trustmarks, seal programmes, the use of corporate privacy officers, private sector enforcement programmes, and the like, as described further in the questionnaire.

Among the countries with omnibus privacy legislation are Australia, Austria, Belgium, the Czech Republic, Finland, France, Germany, Italy, Korea, Norway, the Slovak Republic, Sweden, Switzerland, and the United Kingdom. Countries without a single omnibus law include Japan, Mexico, Turkey, and the United States. Legislation is currently being considered in Japan and Turkey. Some countries have sector-specific laws as well. For instance, many European Union (EU) member States have sectoral legislation regarding telecommunications privacy, and Finland has laws on telecommunications, openness in government activities, employment privacy, police data files, and criminal records. The United States has laws that address privacy protection concerning various sectors, such as the privacy of children's information, and financial and medical information. Germany has specific acts relating to online services. Most respondents also have additional forms of legal regulation, such as decrees, ordinances, administrative rules, and case law (for instance, France, Germany, Italy, Sweden, and Switzerland have ordinances or decrees). Case law plays a differing role in various member countries: for example, in the United States it is a major source of law, while French law does not regard it as an independent source of law. In Japan there are various self-regulatory guidelines in place, while in the United Kingdom human rights legislation is of particular relevance. Administrative rules and regulations play an important role in the United States.

The member countries of the EU are all bound by the Data Protection Directive, and the various public law agreements and instruments which the European Commission has entered into (such as the Safe Harbour arrangement, and the model contracts for data transfer). Some European countries are also parties to other EU agreements that include data protection provisions, notably in the area of police co-operation. The same countries and others are also members of the Council of Europe (COE), and are bound by the Convention for the Protection of Individuals with regard to Automatic Processing of Personal Data. Mexico has signed an Economic Partnership, Political Consensus and Co-operation Agreement with the European Union and its member States which establishes commitments to promote the protection of personal data, among other aspects. The respondents also share a commitment to implement various other international instruments (such as the OECD Guidelines on the Protection of Privacy and

Transborder Flows of Personal Data (the OECD Privacy Guidelines), the United Nations Guidelines on Computerised Personal Data Files, and others). With regard specifically to model contracts for data transfer, the decisions of the European Commission on model contracts are applicable in the EU member States and have been implemented by them.

The Czech Republic recommends the use of model contracts. The USCIB has participated in the drafting of the alternative model contracts that the International Chamber of Commerce (ICC) and other business organisations have recently presented to the European Commission for approval. A set of model clauses has also been jointly published by the ICC, European Commission, and COE.

Most countries do not have government-endorsed codes of conduct. In Australia, some industry codes of practice have been lodged with the Privacy Commissioner for approval. In the Slovak Republic, all technological norms are endorsed by a governmental entity, while in Sweden industry organisations may submit codes of conduct to the Data Inspection Board for an opinion and the Board has, so far, issued opinions on two such codes. Japan has created a model for guidelines to be set up by business organisations, and a number of companies have set up guidelines in conformance with the model. In many countries (such as Austria, France, Mexico, and the United States) the use of codes of conduct for privacy protection is encouraged. The majority of respondents mentioned that they have private sector codes of conduct, best practices, seal or trustmark programmes that are either endorsed by a business federation, or widely used by the private sector either generally or in a specific sector. Most of the responses concerned codes of conduct, but some (Germany, Japan and the United States, for example) also mentioned that they had seal or trustmark programmes. The Korean Association of Information and Telecommunications mentioned that they award an 'ePrivacy Mark' to qualified Internet sites that satisfy stringent data protection criteria.

Nearly every respondent mentioned some form of government regulation applicable to the security of Web sites, although in many countries (e.g. Austria, Finland, France, Norway, and Sweden) there is no special legislation dealing solely with Web sites but general data protection or security legislation. In Japan private sector guidelines set forth security parameters for business, and guidelines have also been promulgated by governmental entities. In Mexico there are self-regulating measures in the financial sector that guarantee the security of online services. In the United States, a site's misrepresentation to consumers about its privacy and security practices could be a violation of federal consumer protection law. Additionally, there are statutory provisions and administrative rules on security safeguards applicable to the financial sector.

Respondents indicated that a wide variety of entities are consulted in their countries for information and advice on compliance with the norms identified above. Those with a public independent privacy authority (for instance, Australia, Austria, Belgium and the Czech Republic) indicated that they could be consulted. A number of respondents also mentioned private-sector lawyers and law firms (e.g. Finland). Some mentioned governmental bodies other than privacy commissioners: for instance, in Japan there are 'Information Security Advisers' at each Prefectural Police Headquarters (Local

Police Department) who give information and advice about 'Unauthorised Computer Access Law' and computer crime.

Respondents indicated that governmental authorities responsible for privacy protection can review privacy practices of businesses. This can be based on administrative procedures, reviews based on best practices, software tools, or other means for reviewing the privacy practices followed by businesses engaged in online activities, Japan indicated that there are standard practices in place (such as 'JIS Q 15001') which provide for regular business audits, as well as for a 'Privacy Mark System'. Switzerland mentioned that there is an initiative in the private sector for a labelling and auditing programmes for e-commerce. In the United Kingdom, the British Standards Institute has published an audit manual for self-audit, and has included data protection in its suite of software legal compliance tools. Similar initiatives have been promulgated by industry groups such as the World Wide Web Consortium (W3C); this was mentioned by the United States, which indicated that software tools can help companies translate their privacy policies into a Platform for Privacy Preferences (P3P) machine-readable format and can allow a company to inventory all features on its Web site so it can track and control its privacy risks.

In the German omnibus privacy act, there is a provision on privacy auditing which is to be implemented by more specific legislation. Australia and the United States indicated that they encourage companies to voluntarily engage in self-assessment of their privacy practices. It was noted that, in the particular case of the 'Safe Harbor' frameworks in the United States, participants must assess their practices, either by a third party or by self-assessment. In the Netherlands, the data protection authority has developed auditing tools in co-operation with private organisations (e.g. a self-evaluation method and a framework for privacy audits). In Mexico and Sweden, companies voluntarily engage in such self-assessment. Most countries indicated that self-assessments are not usually made publicly available, with the exception of the United States, where some (but not all) companies make them public. Only in the Slovak Republic is there a legal requirement for self-assessment.

In countries with governmental data protection agencies, such authorities are competent to oversee compliance with norms. Other governmental agencies may also monitor compliance with norms in specific sectors (for instance, in Finland the Finnish Communications Regulatory Authority together with telecommunications operators, the telecommunications equipment industry, and user associations promote privacy protection and information security in telecommunications). In those countries where private sector compliance systems are active (such as Japan and the United States), the entities that run such systems also monitor compliance with them, together with competent governmental agencies. The organisation and powers of governmental regulatory bodies are determined by appropriate legislation.

Private sector oversight entities are usually set up based on agreements entered into by the participants in the system. Governmental bodies have oversight powers as granted to them by law, which typically include carrying out audits, issuing warnings breaches to the appropriate authorities (as in France). Private sector entities tend to have similar powers, which can include responding to complaints and enquiries and expelling offending organisations from the scheme, without, of course, the full panoply of powers available to governmental entities.

Responses indicated that there is an increasing trend on the part of companies to appoint internal Data Protection Officers; in a few countries, there is a legal obligation to do so. The USCIB and United States government say that self-regulatory bodies can offer advice on policy and practices, that over 500 companies now have Chief Privacy Officers who are responsible for ensuring that their companies adhere to existing laws and follow sound privacy practices, and that there now exist umbrella organisations in the private sector to assist companies in developing practices and procedures. The United States also mentioned that entities covered under the Health Insurance Portability and Accountability Act will be required by law to appoint a privacy officer when the Act takes effect in April 2003. Also, in Korea, companies must appoint a company privacy officer who will safeguard information and deal with complaints from data subjects. In the Slovak Republic, if a controller of information systems employs more than five persons, he has to appoint a responsible person or several such persons to carry on the supervision of compliance with statutory provisions in personal data processing.

Finally, in Germany, public and private entities with more than four employees have to appoint a data protection officer. Almost none of the other respondents indicated the presence of a legal requirement for companies to appoint a privacy officer in charge of compliance. However, in Finland, the Data Protection Ombudsman has recommended that companies appoint a privacy officer, as do various self-regulatory programs in Japan and the data protection authorities in Norway,

Switzerland, and the United Kingdom. The law of some member countries (e.g. Germany, the Netherlands and Sweden) exempt companies that appoint a company privacy officer from certain legal obligations.

Notification of data processing to an oversight entity is mandatory in Austria, Belgium, the Czech Republic, Finland, France, Italy, Norway, the Slovak Republic, Sweden, Switzerland, and the United Kingdom. However, even in such countries, certain exceptions apply, or notification may apply only to certain situations. For instance, in Sweden notification is not required if a personal data representative has been appointed or if the processing takes place with the individual's consent. Also, in Japan the TRUSTe Japan seal programme requires the notification of processing to an oversight department. Notification of data processing by banks may be required in Mexico under certain circumstances.

Technological solutions to protect privacy are implemented to a limited extent only, although some member countries (such as Japan, the United Kingdom, and the United States) indicated that the use of technical standards (such as P3P) to ensure compliance is expanding. The UK Information Commissioner promotes the use of privacy enhancing technologies, while in the United States there are many such tools widely available on the Internet (including P3P) but it is unclear how many businesses or consumers take advantage of them. The German Ministry of Economy and Technology has a programme to encourage the anonymous use of online technology. The Netherlands indicated that the Dutch government has committed itself to the use of privacy-enhancing-technologies in new public data processing systems.

However, these initiatives remain exceptions. Otherwise, the use of technology to protect privacy was mentioned in the context of security. In Austria, as in other countries, the use of firewalls, anti-virus software and other safety precautions is standard, and the law requires certain data security measures but does not specify the exact techniques that are to be used. Finland indicated that the situation in companies varies to a great extent depending mainly on the size and partly on the field of the company. Japan stated that SSL and other encryption technologies are used to protect sensitive information such as credit card numbers, as is the case in Turkey.

Every OECD member country has at least one government authority, which can enforce privacy norms. Italy mentioned that under the law, data subjects can always turn to data controllers to exercise their rights in the event of a dispute. Japan, the United Kingdom, and the United States say that data subjects may also be able to turn to a self-regulatory scheme, in cases where one is applicable. Most respondents indicated the possibility of obtaining judicial or administrative relief based on a case brought in court or with governmental authorities, such as monetary compensation for damages, injunctive relief, erasure of data or blocking of processing. Austria say that most privacy claims against private entities must be brought before the courts, but that many claims regarding privacy issues are resolved through other legal instrumentse OECD member countries.

The United States say that the Federal Trade Commission (FTC) could sue companies who misrepresent their privacy policies, through administrative procedures or through the courts, and could obtain injunctions and monetary redress for complaints are brought before data protection or consumer protection authorities, which may then investigate the complaint and take appropriate action, which may include imposing penalties or referring the case to the courts or criminal authorities. In some countries (such as Italy) the data subject should first make an application to the data controller before applying for relief to the data protection authorities, whereas in others (Sweden, for example) the data subject may turn directly to the authorities or go first to the data controller. As Japan pointed out, self-regulatory bodies have their own procedures for handling complaints.

Online filing of complaints is possible in a number of member countries (for example, Australia, Austria, France, Germany, Japan, Sweden, and the United States). Norway indicated that, while online filing was not formally provided for, it was used in practice (i.e. data subjects would often send complaints or inquiries to data protection authorities by e-mail). The United Kingdom is working on an online filing system. Mexico specifically noted that the Federal Consumer Protection Agency (Profeco) takes part in an international programmes conducted within the framework of the International Marketing Supervision Network (IMSN) which has resulted in the establishment of a Web site to gather and share complaints about cross-border electronic commerce. In the United States, the FTC administers the IMSN website programme and also maintains its own agency Web site to allow consumers to criticise on privacy complaints, including those relating to Internet representations and e-commerce transactions.

Alternative dispute resolution (ADR) mechanisms for privacy-related disputes, such as arbitration and mediation, are in use in only a few countries, such as

Austria, Korea and the United States. France indicated that a number of such schemes are now being developed by the European Commission. Italy indicated that ADR schemes are used, but that they are not specifically focused on privacy disputes. Such mechanisms are now being developed in Japan. In Germany some trustmark providers may offer such schemes.

Only a few countries indicated that auditing of privacy practices is used as a method of enforcement. In Finland the Data Protection Ombudsman has the right to audit personal data registers and the Finnish Communications Regulatory Authority has the right to audit telecom operators' activities. The French Data Protection Authority (CNIL) has also used online surveys to inventory the practices of Web sites. Auditing by self-regulatory bodies is used in Japan and the United States, and voluntary audits are used in Mexico. Auditing may also be a kind of mandatory enforcement mechanism used by governmental agencies, for example in Sweden and the United States. Some of the local data protection authorities in Germany are presently using software tools to conduct audits of Web sites. Many respondents mentioned that security audits are often used to review the security of information systems and computer networks.

Most countries stated that the public or private sectors had undertaken campaigns to educate the public as to their privacy rights. Among the methods used are speeches and meetings; media interviews; disseminating copies of publications; information on the Web sites of privacy authorities, the publication of annual programmes by privacy authorities; the creation of online 'privacy toolboxes' by companies; and self-regulatory schemes which tell users how they can limit disclosure of their personal information, what choices they have about how such information is used and shared, and under what circumstances they can access it.

No respondents have specific legal requirements to post online privacy policies. However, in many member countries data controllers (including operators of Web sites) have legal obligations to inform the data subject of the processing of his data (including such matters as access rights etc), and this obligation can be satisfied through an online privacy policy. Many government and private sector schemes also encourage companies to post online privacy policies. When a privacy policy is posted, it may need to include certain mandatory information, such as the identity of the data controller and the purpose of the processing.

Intellectual Property Protection (IPP)

There has been a lot of controversy on the role of intellectual property protection (IPP) regime especially the patent system in fostering innovation, technology and industrial development of a country. IPP is expected to encourage innovation by rewarding the inventor with the grant of monopoly rights over the commercial exploitation of their inventions for a specified period. On the other hand, strong IPP regime may inhibit diffusion of knowledge and even technology development in the countries that are technology followers. The history suggests that countries have fine-tuned their IPP regimes as per their developmental requirements. Typically, countries in Asia and in other regions have had softer IPP regimes in the early stages of their development and these regimes have been strengthened as the countries developed and became significant producers of innovations and new technology themselves. In particular, some countries, such as India, have successfully developed cost-effective processes to produce life saving drugs with softer patent regimes. This enabled the national health system to provide affordable medicines to masses of poorer people. Against this backdrop, the on-going attempt to harmonize and strengthen the IPP regimes worldwide, as a part of the TRIPs Agreement, is widely seen to be adversely affecting the technological activity in developing countries by choking the knowledge spillovers from industrialized countries to developing countries. Furthermore, the implementation of the provisions of TRIPs Agreement threatens the access and affordability of poor people to lifesaving drugs by pushing up their prices. This has been highlighted by the recent controversy regarding the availability of AIDS drugs in South Africa.

The global technology generation or innovative activity is known to be highly concentrated in a handful of technologically advanced developed countries. The top ten countries account for as much as 84 per cent of global resources spent on R&D activity annually, they control 94 per cent of the technological output in terms of patents taken out in the US, and receive 91 per cent of global cross-border royalties and technology license fees. Hence, the concentration in terms of technological output is even more uneven than for technological inputs. The control over technology is reflected in their 74 per cent share of global FDI outflows. The relative position of countries in terms of different indicators varies. It is curious to find, for instance, that Japan accounts for 17-18 per cent of global R&D expenditure and US patents, but shares only 8.6 per cent of global technological receipts (and only 3 per cent of FDI outflows). Similarly, The Netherlands and Switzerland command a much higher proportion of global royalties than their share of R&D expenditure or patents. The discrepancy between the share in technological activity and returns in terms of royalties could be on account of different focus of the technological effort of different countries. The technological effort of Japanese corporations seems to be geared towards obtaining competitiveness of their products in domestic and export markets more than for supporting the transfer of technology and production.

However, the bulk of this 5.7 per cent share is accounted for Taiwan (which accounts for 2.54 %) and South Korea (with 1.86 %), although a few countries e.g. Israel, China, Hong Kong, Singapore, India are showing an increasing trend of patenting in the US. The rise of innovative activity in Taiwan and Korea is not only reflected in increasing number of US patents owned but also in emerging technology exports which are as yet small in value terms but have grown rapidly over the past few years. Therefore these countries together with Japan make important cases for analyzing the role played by IPRs in their technology development.

There are three ways that the strength of the IPR regime could affect economic growth indirectly: IPR regime may affect the innovative activity that in turn is the source of total factor productivity improvements and thus contributes to growth. The IPR regime could affect the inflows of FDI and technology transfers and which could impinge upon the growth. Given the international dimension of IPR regimes, there could be implications for international trade of countries, for instance, on the ability of countries to export certain goods. Finally, the changes in IPR regimes may imply some redistribution of income between the countries and between communities within the country.

There are a few studies that have addressed the issue of effect of IPR regime on growth directly. However, the observed effects could be subject to the causality problem as developed countries are likely to have stronger IPRs regime than the poorer ones. In other words, the level of development is likely to be a determinant for strength of IPR regime rather than the other way round. Ginarte and Park in a study covering 110 countries for the period 1960-90 corroborated that either the level of economic development or factors correlated with it e.g. the level of R&D activity, market environment, and international integration explain the strength of patent protection provided by countries.

Furthermore, Maskus and Penubarti find the relationship between IPR protection and level of development to be non-linear suggesting that patent protection tends to decline in strength as economies move beyond the poorest stage into a middle-income stage in which they have greater abilities to imitate new technologies. Therefore, the finding of Gould and Gruben that found a significant positive effect of the strength of patent protection on growth of 79 countries (after controlling for investment rates and human capital development) particularly for open economies could be subject to causality bias. The indirect nature of the possible effect of IPRs on growth is also confirmed by Park and Ginarte. Thompson and Rushing empirically observe that universally imposed minimum standards for patent protection are not likely to contribute to increased growth in developing countries. However, stronger patent protection could contribute to economic growth rates once a particular level of development has been achieved. In a further refinement to their earlier results, Thampson and Rushing find that patent protection could be positively associated with improvement in total factor productivity, and hence growth, in wealthy or developed countries. Therefore, the IPR regime could affect economic growth and development through other variables such as innovative activity, FDI inflows and technology transfers. In what follows the evidence on the effect of IPR regime on innovative activity and FDI and technology transfer and trade is reviewed.

The main argument offered in favour of tighter and more stringent laws to protect intellectual property and patent rights is to provide better conditions for appropriability of innovations. However, the existing empirical literature suggests that the effectiveness of patent protection varies from industry to industry and is most effective only in chemical and pharmaceutical industries. A study by Mansfield showed that around 65 per cent of pharmaceutical and 30 per cent of chemical inventions would not have taken place but for patent protection. In the case of most other industries patent protection was not important. In the case of most of the engineering industries, and in particular, electrical & electronic goods, and instruments etc. patent protection was not found to be essential for the introduction of inventions. This finding was confirmed by most of the subsequent studies. For instance, a survey conducted by Levin et al. showed that product patents were found to be highly effective as means of appropriating returns only in five of 130 narrowly defined lines of businesses. These five included drugs, organic chemicals, pesticides. Shankerman in an analysis of French patent renewal data for the period 1969-72, concludes that while patents may be a significant source of returns to innovative enterprises, they are not the major ones. The main reason for limited effectiveness of patents is the ability of competitors to legally 'invent around' patents.

Gallini finds that longer patent life pushes the rivals to invent around the patent inventions. Hence, optimal patent life are sufficiently short to discourage imitation. These studies also revealed that secrecy to be more effective than patents in protecting process innovations. Besides in the case of several high technology industries like aerospace and industrial machinery the complexity of the products made reverse engineering very costly and imitation difficult even without patent protection. Hall using a game theoretic model of a R&D race to analyze the effect of weakening patents has on the timing and profitability of R&D, found that in general, a second innovation (or inventing around) would occur later than it would have if the IPR policy had not been weakened. Scherer and Weisburst examined the impact of strengthening of pharmaceutical patent protection in Italy since 1978. They concluded that the regime change had little or no impact on the trend of inflation-adjusted R&D expenditures or on the introduction of new chemical entities. Hence, they expressed their scepticism on the prospect of the trend of lengthening of patent protection with TRIPs Agreement in significantly raising innovative activity especially in developing countries.

Cohen and Levinthal, in their comprehensive model explaining R&D intensity, considered technological opportunity as well as appropriability as determinants and also assessed the net impact of the spillovers of R&D. Technological opportunity is a function of technological and research output in that area as well as the output of other R&D units which the patent owners wish to protect by reducing the spillover effects. On the other hand the spillover effect is one of the notable inputs to R&D. The analysis showed that the positive absorption incentive associated with spillovers seemed to increase relative to the negative appropriability incentive in the case of many industries.

A more detailed analysis conducted to examine whether the spillovers on balance actually encouraged R&D in some industries found that in the case of chemicals and electrical and electronics, R&D intensities increased with spillovers. Therefore, the available evidence does not indicate that further tightening of patent laws would increase expenditures on R&D. On the contrary, strong patent laws could even hurt subsequent R&D effort by restricting spillovers.

In this context it might also be useful to recall that Schumpeter had argued for a short-term monopoly profits to encourage innovation and not for a legal institutionalized monopoly position. He had emphasized that monopoly offered no cushion to sleep on and hence the temporary state of monopoly resulting from the possession of a new technology. In the medium and long term the firm would be subject to the threat of competition and the advent of better or improved products from rivals. Hence, the need for the firm to safeguard its market position through continuous innovative activities. It was this process that prevented the original creator of a new technology from being complacent and prompted the monopolist to be constantly creative. A legal protection as provided by the patent system for a rather longer term of twenty years, therefore, erodes the threat of potential competition and hence, the need for continuous improvement.

The importance of foreign R&D spillovers as a determinant of R&D activity could be even more critical in developing countries where much of the R&D activity is of an adaptive nature. A number of studies have empirically demonstrated the ability of rather weaker intellectual property rights in stimulating domestic innovative activity in developing countries to absorb spillovers of foreign R&D. Fikkert in a study of Indian enterprises found evidence of their R&D activity absorbing considerable foreign R&D spillovers facilitated by weak Indian patent regime. He suggested that a 'weak patent regime may allow spillovers simultaneously to promote R&D and to have a positive direct effect on productivity' and concluded that the adoption of a 'stronger patent regime may not be optimal from either the short- or long-run perspectives'. Similarly, Kumar and Saqib found Indian chemical industry enterprises to be among the more innovative ones in the Indian industry. They attributed this to the weak patent laws viz. absence of product patents in India which enabled Indian enterprises to undertake alternative process development.

The importance of spillovers from innovative activity in developed countries for domestic technological effort in developing countries facilitated by softer IPRs has also been corroborated by other studies. Haksar estimated marginal products of R&D and technology imports and their spillover effects using the Reserve Bank of India data for 642 Indian firms distributed across 65 industries for 1975-1990 period. His finds both local R&D and disembodied technology imports generating positive spillovers. In the pharmaceutical industry the return to R&D were found to be particularly large and was explained in terms of highly successful adaptive R&D effort of Indian firms directed at development of alternative processes of known drugs made possible by the absence of patents on pharmaceutical products.

The above review of literature suggests that the evidence on the role of IPRs as a determinant of innovative activity is quite weak. In fact stronger IPRs may actually affect the innovative activity adversely by chocking the absorption of knowledge spillovers that are important determinants of innovative activity. Mazzoleni and Nelson is a survey of theoretical and empirical studies also conclude that 'there is reason for concern that the present movement towards stronger patent protection may hinder rather than stimulate technological and economic progress.'

Technology Licensing and Trade

There has been a considerable controversy on the role of intellectual property protection in determining inward FDI flows and their effect on technology licensing and trade. In the OLI theory of international operations of firm, exports, FDI and arm's length technology licensing are considered as alternative modes of servicing a foreign market by firms. Stronger protection increases the value or revenue productivity of a firm's intellectual property such as technology, brand and trade names. Stronger protection should help exporters by making imitation and counterfeiting more difficult. The favourable effect of stronger IPRs in foreign countries on exports has generally been confirmed empirically by a number of studies.

However the effect of IPR strength on FDI and licensing is not that straight forward. By reducing the transaction cost of transfer of knowledge by MNEs to foreign countries, stronger protection may encourage arm's length licensing of the knowledge and reduce the need for undertaking FDI. On the other hand, it has been argued that poor IPR regime tends to adversely affect the investment climate and hence the probability of MNE investments. Relatively little empirical verification of these contentions that has been made has generally shown an insignificant influence of the extent of IPP on inward FDI. Frischtak and Bosworth did not find a significant role of IPRs in influencing the pattern of FDI and technology transfers respectively. Ferrantino found no discernible impact of a country's adherence to IPR agreements on the arm's length exports or subsidiary sales (i.e. FDI) of US firms. But subsidiaries in countries adhering to IPRs had a greater chance of sourcing more components from the US than from the host countries.

The affiliates in countries belonging to the Paris Convention are also likely to have higher payments of royalties and licence fees than others. The greater dependence on parents for sourcing components also creates greater potential for transfer pricing. Since the 'U.S. is generally a low tax regime compared to LDCs, this suggests that strong international IPRs may indirectly cause a diversion of tax revenue from LDCs to the US treasury'. Kondo found no consistently significant relationship between the strength of patent laws in terms of four alternative indicators and the levels of and changes in US FDI in a sample of 33 countries over a 15 year period. Lee and Mansfield, on the other hand, in a sample of 14 countries (observations pooled over three years) find the perceived weakness of intellectual property protection adversely affecting the volume as well as the composition of US FDI inflows to the countries. However, given the small size of sample, a rather subjective measurement of intellectual property regime (based on firm's perception), and low t-values of the coefficients, the findings could be considered only as indicative unless replicated in larger samples. In a study covering 27 less developed countries for the period 1975-90, Sayoum finds that IPR factors to be significant in explaining variation in inward FDI and the effect was particularly strong for emerging countries. Mascus found that strength of patent protection had a negative effect on the sales and assets of affiliates of US MNEs, although only the coefficient was statistically significant only in the second case. However, the impact of patent protection affiliate sales and assets was positive and significant in the case of developing countries sub-sample.

The strength of patent protection in explaining the sales and value addition of affiliates of US and Japanese affiliates in 74 countries in seven broad branches of industry and at three points of time in the framework of an extended model of location of foreign production. The strength of patent protection regime although with a positive sign never had a statistically significant coefficient for affiliate sales or value added in the case of US MNEs. In the case of Japanese MNEs, the results were sensitive to inclusion of dummy variables identifying the two tiers of Asian NIEs. The coefficient of patent rights was not significantly different from zero in a full sample test when the regional dummies are not included. When the Asian NIEs are separated with the dummy variables, than the coefficient of patent rights becomes statistically significant with a positive sign. This suggests that Japanese MNEs have tended to overlook the relatively weaker IPR regime prevailing in the East and South East Asian countries for their outward investments. Outside East and Southeast Asia, Japanese investments are concentrated in the

European Union and North America-countries having stronger IPR regime. Hence, one gets a positive significant coefficient. In the sub-sample estimations for Japanese affiliate sales in developing countries, patent rights variable comes up with a significant coefficient with a negative sign. That could be explained in terms of high concentration of Japanese investment in developing countries in those countries that have weaker IPR regime.

The coefficient of the strength of patent protection is never significantly different from zero while explaining the value added of US and Japanese affiliates. The strength of patent regime does not appear to be a significant factor in determining the patterns of US or Japanese FDI. Some further analysis of the same data set at the level of seven broad sectors, currently in progress and reported in Kumar suggests that strength of patent protection does not influence the patterns of US affiliate sales in any of the seven branches of manufacturing except the miscellaneous industry where it had a significant but negative coefficient. Smith finds that foreign patent rights increase US affiliate sales (i.e. FDI) as well as licenses. However, the effect is larger in the case of arm' length licensing than for FDI. These conclusions are consistent with those of Yang and Mascus who find that patent rights promote arm's length trade and they have a less significant effect on internalized technology transfers viz. FDI.

The issue of IPR protection links more directly with R&D activity in the context of globalization of R&D activity of MNEs. MNEs may be apprehensive of locating their key R&D centres in countries with weak patent regimes. However, where the overseas R&D is directed to local adaptations and to providing other support to the local production of the MNE, and not directed to new product development, the patent regime may not be of much consequence to it. Kumar in a study explaining R&D intensity of affiliates of US MNEs in 54 countries in 1977, 1982, and 1989, found that strength of patent protection had a significant positive influence on R&D intensity of affiliates located in developed countries and has a negative coefficient in a developing country sub-sample which is not statistically significant.

Thus stronger patent protection does not appear to be a prerequisite even for R&D investments by MNEs in developing countries. Kumar provides case study evidence suggesting that MNEs have been locating R&D centres, R&D joint ventures and contracting research in India in the field of chemicals and pharmaceuticals despite the patent regime not recognizing product patents in these sectors. Therefore, availability of abundant trained low cost human resources and scale of ongoing R&D in their own fields appear to be more important considerations for location of R&D in developing countries than the strength of IPR regime.

These hypotheses were verified in a more recent study that explained R&D intensity of affiliates of US and Japanese MNEs in 74 countries in seven branches of industry and at three points of time, 1982, 1989, and 1994. This study found that the strength of patent protection offered by the country remained statistically insignificant in explaining R&D intensity of US and Japanese affiliates throughout. The bulk of the variation in R&D intensity was explained by the abundance of R&D manpower and its relative cost, scale of national technological effort and technological capability of the host country especially in the field of the affiliate.

It would appear from the above that the contention that stronger norms of IPR protection will facilitate greater inflows of FDI in the country is rather weak in either theoretical or empirical terms. The theory suggests that stronger IPRs may tilt the balance between exports, FDI, and licensing in favour of exports and arm's length licensing. The empirical evidence has been mixed generally supporting no strong effect of the strength of patent protection on FDI inflows, their composition and even overseas R&D activity of MNEs. As Mascus puts it, if strong IPRs were able to provide sufficient incentives for firms to invest in a country, 'recent FDI flows to developing economies would have gone mainly to sub-Saharan Africa and Eastern Europe. In contrast, China, Brazil and other high-growth, large-market developing economies with weak protection would not have attracted nearly as much FDI'.

IPRs in Asian countries

The rapid and sustained growth and development in the East Asian economies, viz. Japan; South Korea, Taiwan, Hong Kong and Singapore, Malaysia, Thailand, and Indonesia and China, generally termed as the 'East Asian Miracle', has attracted a large volume of literature. The growth rate of per capita income over the 1960-90 for these economies averaged over 5.5 per cent, making it the fastest growing region in the world sustaining such rates of growth over such a long span of time. Japan and Asian nies have been able to expand their share in world exports from 8 per cent in 1965 to 13 per cent in 1980 and 18 per cent in 1990, suggesting that their exports have expanded much faster than any other region's. Their share in world's manufactured exports has grown from 11 to 21 per cent over the same period. In particular rapid transformation of Korea and Taiwan from technologically backward and poor economies into affluent and relatively modern economies by early 1990s has been truly remarkable.

Some analysts have attempted to downplay the East Asian achievement as a result of factor accumulation along the production function. However, since then a number of studies have corroborated that a substantial proportion of East Asian growth was contributed by growth of total factor productivity (TFP) and it was not a result of merely factor accumulation. The total factor productivity growth in Japan, Korea, Taiwan, Hong Kong and Thailand has averaged between 2 to 4 per cent per year over 1960-89 thus contributing over a third of the growth of output!

A large volume of literature has also been concerned with the explanation of the rapid TFP growth in the East Asian countries. It is now widely accepted that the assimilation of foreign technology was a 'critical component of the Asian Miracle'. There seems to be a general consensus that the East Asian success owes a lot, in general, to their ability to imitate, absorb, assimilate and replicate foreign innovations. Kim highlights the role of 'duplicative imitation' in the Korean industries initially in the light industries such as textiles, toys, consumer electronics in the 1960s and in such heavy industries such as automobiles, steel, shipbuilding and machinery in the 1970s. Hobday provides case studies of firm level learning in Korea as well as other East Asian countries. Singh and Trieu provide econometric evidence suggesting that R&D expenditures in Japan, South Korea and Taiwan have contributed to TFP growth.

The existing evidence on the role of IPRs regime in promoting growth is largely anecdotal. Although the literature is not explicit in acknowledging its role, the soft intellectual property protection regime adopted by these countries in the period of duplicative imitation or reverse engineering has played and important role in facilitating the firm level technological learning. Below we attempt to put together some evidence for Japan, Korea and Taiwan on the role weak IPRs regime adopted by these countries have facilitated their technological and economic development.

Japan

Japan is known to have greatly benefited from intellectual property generated in other developed countries in the early stages its development. In fact the two international treaties on the IPRs viz. the Paris Convention for industrial property and the Berne Convention for copyrights "were negotiated, in part because of frustration over alleged infringements in the 'newly industrialising countries' of the day, such as the United States and Japan". Furthermore, in Japan the patent protection has been designed with an ultimate objective of contributing to the 'development of industry' and not as an end by itself. In tune with this objective it has contained several features that have helped the absorption of spillovers of foreign inventive activity by domestic enterprises. For instance, although Japanese Patent System (JPS) was established in 1885 by the Patent Monopoly Ordinance that was replaced by the Patent Ordinance of 1888, the food, beverage, pharmaceutical products and chemical compounds were excluded from the scope of patent protection until 1975 to facilitate the process innovations. In 1905 the Utility Model Law was introduced to provide protection to adaptations or improvements over the imported machinery or equipment by domestic inventors that were considered too minor to be patented primarily. As many as 99.9 per cent of utility models have been granted to Japanese nationals over the 1905- 79 period. Furthermore, the JPS provides for protection of industrial designs which only needed to demonstrate novelty and not inventiveness.

The utility models and industrial designs have allowed Japanese firms to receive protection on technologies that were 'only slightly modified from the original invention'. JPS also employs the first-to-file principle rather than the first-to-invent principle incorporated in the US law, pre-grant disclosure that lays open or publishes the patent applications for inspection or opposition for eighteen months, provides for compulsory license if a patent has not been worked (i.e. used in manufacture) in Japan continuously for more than three years or in public interest, and required the patent applications to be limited to a single narrow claim. All these features have been designed to favour adpatations by domestic enterprises. That they have been used to encourage technology adaptations by domestic entrepreneurs is clear from the fact that in 1980 Japan had awarded 49000 utility models to its nationals compared to just 533 to foreigners. Similarly Japanese nationals were granted 31000 industrial design patents vis-à-vis 600 to foreigners. There have also been complaints of discrimination by JPO and foreign applicants appear to face longer pendency periods than do domestic applicants in Japan.

Mascus and McDaniel in a systematic quantitative study have found that the above features namely utility models, design patents, compulsory licenses, first-to-apply, narrow claims, among others, that make JPS considerably weaker than the US patent system, for instance, have facilitated absorption, transfer and diffusion of technology by allowing reverse engineering and contributed to the TFP growth during the period 1960-93. The scope of patent system was expanded to cover chemical and pharmaceutical products only in 1975. Kotabe attributes the regime change to the growing international pressure. However, it was probably motivated by the realization that by 1970s, Japanese enterprises had developed their technological capability adequately and hence needed protection for their own innovative activity. In October 1970 the Japan Patent Association surveyed its member firms on whether they favoured introduction of chemical product patents. About 60 per cent of the respondents favoured product patents and only 9 per cent opposed. With this strong support from the industry, the Japanese government began the process of amending Japanese patent law to provide for product patents for chemicals and pharmaceuticals. The amendment was adopted by the Diet in May 1975 and became effective from January 1976.

South Korea

South Korea adopted the patent legislation only in 1961. The Korean patent law was amended in 1981 to conform with the Paris Convention that provided for multiple claims for related inventions in a single application. However, the scope of patenting did not cover patenting of products and processes to manufacture food products, chemical substances and pharmaceuticals. The US government initiated an investigation on Korea under Section 301 of the Trade Act threatening trade sanctions on Korean exports for its failure to provide protection to US products. That pushed Korea to strengthen its IPR regime. The revised patent, copyright, and software legislation was passed by the National Assembly on 31

December 1986 and became effective in July 1987. The new law extended product patent protection to new chemical and pharmaceutical products, adopted a comprehensive copyright law, and extended copyright protection to computer software.

The patent term was also extended from 12 to 15 years. Korea has also followed an IPR regime that facilitated adaptations and imitative duplication of foreign technologies by domestic enterprises through utility models and industrial designs. It is evident from the fact that 92 to 95 per cent of all utility models and industrial designs have been granted to its nationals. The delibrate softening of IPR regime by the government to facilitate imitation by domestic enterprises has been acknowledged in the literature on Korean technological capability. Lee, for instance, observes that during the imitation stage, the 'government tried to minimize IPR protection to help domestic firms use foreign intellectual property. Laws and regulations were formulated in such a way as to meet minimal international standards. Furthermore, enforcement of the law was less than strict'. Kim provides highly illustrative case studies of several industries documenting firm level successes in absorbing technology and other knowledge with the help of duplicative imitation or reverse engineering and gradually emerging as innovators in their own right. The softer patent regime adopted by the country facilitated this process of reverse engineering. La Croix and Kawaura in an event study of the effect of the new patent law on the market valuation of Korean pharmaceutical firms listed on the stock exchange found a cumulative decline of -74 per cent over the 14 months period. Korea's ability to absorb foreign innovative activity through duplicative imitation has helped it to grow rapidly during the 1960-1980s. The real

GDP expanded by 9.5 per cent per year during the 1965-1980 period and by 8.6 per cent during 1980-87 period. Despite the new Patents Act of 1986 according product patents for chemicals and pharmaceuticals, Korea continued on the priority watch list of the US government under Special 301 till 1993 for enforcement concerns. In February 1993 Korea launched a comprehensive new plan to strengthen IPRs protection and enforcement followed by a new Patent Act in 1995. Nevertheless, Korea has often been regarded as being weak in protecting IPRs.

In view of the role played by soft patent regime in Korea's development, Kim infers that current trend of strengthening of IPR protection will pre-empt duplicative imitation of foreign technologies by developing countries of today. Reverse engineering of foreign products for duplicative imitation will be more difficult and costly for developing countries than it was for Korea in the 1960s and 1970s. China, for instance, faces enormous pressure from the United States to honour IPRs which Japan, Korea and Taiwan did not face in their early industrialization stage'.

Taiwan

Taiwan has also employed a weak IPR policy to facilitate local absorption of foreign knowledge through reverse engineering on the lines of Japan and South Korea. In fact Taiwan's government seem to openly encourage counterfeiting as strategy to develop local industries. In the mid-1980s an estimated 60 per cent of world's pirated or counterfeit goods were allegedly originating in Taiwan. Wade documents a number of cases of government's tacit approval of counterfeiting. In a late 1970s case, several factories were found to be manufacturing circuit fuse breakers with forged Westinghouse and Mitsubishi labels. When Mitsubishi complained to the authorities, the firms were fined all of US$600.

The government publicly denied that this was a serious case, while privately saying that "political factors" made it impossible to take tough action. Those political factors were the adamant opposition of most Taiwan firms and industry associations to any signs of tough enforcement, since they saw themselves as handsome beneficiaries of non-enforcement. And the government itself tended to view counterfeiting as a shortcut to industrial success. As recently as 1983 an unattributed government document entitled "Intellectual Property Rights Protection, a Republic of China Perspective," said with remarkable candor, "The R.O.C. government has viewed imitation as a necessary process in the evolution of human civilization and believed that commercial counterfeiting is an inevitable phenomenon in most developing countries. Local officials were cognizant of the negative aspects of counterfeiting although they made little effort to accommodate overseas interests or enhance domestic enforcement efforts when such aspects were seen to be outweighed by the positive development of the industrial base.

Lax treatment of IPRs in Taiwan attracted the attention of the US government. In March 1983, the US government instituted bilateral consultations on IPRs with Taiwan. As a result of growing US pressure, Taiwan amended its copyright law in 1985 to strengthen penalties for piracy, provide criteria for recognizing foreign firms' standing before the Taiwanese judiciary in copyright cases, and extend protection specifically to new media, including software. This followed enactment of a new patent law in 1986 extending protection to chemicals and pharmaceutical products. However, these legislations and their enforcement were considered inadequate by the US government. Under heavy pressure from the US Taiwan promulgated its new Patent Law on January 21, 1994 that allows patents on food, beverages, micro-organisms, and new uses for products, all of which were previously excluded under the government's social policy. In addition the duration for new patents was extended from 15 years to 20 years.

Like Japan and Korea, Taiwan also provides for utility models (for 12 years duration under the new law) and design patents (term 10 years under new law). However, many concerns have continued to remain. These include elimination of imprisonment penalties for patent infringement while they continue for violations of utility models and design patents primarily held by Taiwan nationals. There is a provision for patent marking under which a patent owner who fails to mark the patent certificate number on the patented article or packaging cannot claim damages from infringement.

The East Asian countries viz. Japan, Korea and Taiwan have absorbed substantial amount of technological learning under weak IPR protection regime during the early phases. These patent regimes facilitated the absorption of innovation and knowledge generated abroad by their indigenous firms. They have also encouraged minor adaptations and incremental innovations on the foreign inventions by domestic enterprises and developed a patent culture through utility models and design patents. As the local technological capabilities matured and the domestic industry sought stronger protection for guarding their own inventions, the IPR regime was strengthened in Japan in mid-1970s. In the other two countries, the IPR regime had to be strengthened under US pressure.

In the chemicals and pharmaceuticals it did not prove a constraint as the process patents in the absence of product patents essentially served the purpose of encouraging process adaptive activity of domestic firms. As a result, the domestic chemicals and pharmaceutical industries have developed in their capabilities considerably over the past three decades. However, in the engineering industries and others, there was not a mechanism for encouraging minor adaptations of domestic firms. This difference could perhaps explain not so encouraging performance of Indian enterprises in other industries. Furthermore, IPR regime is only one of the determinants of the technological capability building. The domestic technological effort in absorbing the foreign technologies and innovations in East Asian countries has been vastly more substantive and has been sustained over a much longer period compared to India that attempted to build capabilities with softer patent regime only since the mid-1970s. Before this India's patent regime was comparable to those prevailing in the developed countries.

India

India had inherited The Patents and Designs Act 1911 from the colonial times that provided for protection of all inventions except those relating to atomic energy and a patent term of 16 years from the date of application. However, a few domestic chemical and pharmaceutical enterprises that tried to develop their own technology in the 1960s ran into trouble with foreign patent owners. A number of cases highlighted that foreign patent owners were neither using their patents for domestic manufacture nor allowing them to be used by local firms.

That led to a build-up of pressure in the late 1960s for a new patent law. Desai in a questionnaire survey of 53 firms conducted in 1969 found that by and large foreign firms were against any liberalization of patent laws, Indian firms were not against patents but wanted greater access to patented know-how especially when patent owners not allowing their patents to be used. The conflict of views was sharper in chemicals and pharmaceuticals where patents had been used to prevent entry of Indian firms. Therefore, a new Patents Act was adopted in 1970 that reduced the scope of patentability in food, chemicals and pharmaceuticals to only processes and not products. Since virtually any chemical compound can be made by a variety of processes, the scope of patent protection was greatly reduced. The term of process patents was reduced to 7 years in food, drugs and chemicals and to 14 years for other products. The compulsory licenses could be issued after three years. The Indian Patents Act of 1970 has continued to govern the IPR regime in India over the past 30 years except for recent amendments brought to provide for exclusive marketing rights (EMRs) in tune with India's obligations under WTO's TRIPs Agreement.

India joined the Paris Convention and the Patent Cooperation Treaty only in 1999. India has a ten years transition to provide product patents viz. till the end of 2004. It is by now widely recognized that the abolition of product patents in chemicals and pharmaceuticals has facilitated the development of local technological capability in chemicals and pharmaceutical industry by enabling the domestic firms in their process innovative activity. A number of quantitative studies have shown that the innovative activity of Indian domestic enterprises was facilitated by the softer patent regime under the 1970 Act. The gradual build up of technological capability of Indian enterprises is visible from a rising trend of residents in patent ownership in India.

Improved technological capability is also reflected in terms of the ability of India to raise her share in patents granted by the US patents office from 0.02 per cent in 1977-87 period to 0.06 per cent during 1996-2000. Although still having marginal share in the US patent grants, India has not fared badly compared to other developing countries. In 1998, it ranked seventh amongst all developing countries in terms of the magnitude of US patents obtained, behind Taiwan, South Korea and Israel-the three leading nations-but ahead of Brazil, China and Mexico. Interestingly, in the chemicals sector-which accounts for the bulk of all patents-and in biotechnology-one of the cutting edge sectors-India ranks fourth amongst developing countries. Moreover, in biotechnology, the gap between India and countries ahead of it is not large.

In particular, the rapid evolution of Indian pharmaceutical industry since the mid-1970s highlights the fact that weak IPRs regime could be instrumental in building local capabilities even in a poor country such as India. In what follows we take a look at some indicators of evolution of technological capability of Indian pharmaceutical enterprises. In 1970 much of the country's pharmaceutical consumption was met by imports and the bulk of domestic production of formulations was dominated by MNE subsidiaries. Of the top ten firms by retail sales in 1970 only two were domestic firms and the others were MNE subsidiaries. In 1996 six of the top ten firms in the industry are Indian firms. By 1991, domestic firms accounted for 70 per cent of the bulk drugs production and 80 per cent of formulations produced in the country.

The increasing technological capability is reflected in terms of rising exports of drugs and pharmaceuticals. With their cost effective process innovations, Indian companies have emerged as competitive suppliers in the world of a large number of generic drugs that are now outside the patent protection. That has resulted in a steady growth of India's exports of drugs and pharmaceuticals. Thus the industry has evolved from being one being highly import dependent to one that generates increasing export surplus for the country. The faster growth of pharmaceutical exports has resulted in their share in India's exports rising from 0.55 per cent in 1970-71 to over 4 per cent by the 1999/00. India ranks second after China among developing countries in export of pharmaceuticals and is ahead of such technologically advanced countries as Mexico, South Korea, Brazil, Israel.

Indian exports of pharmaceuticals received a boost in the late 1980s when a number of drugs went off the patents and Indian companies manufacturing them with cost-effective processes entered the international markets after obtaining FDA approval. Therefore, in the late 1980s, as much as 61 per cent of India's pharmaceutical exports comprised bulk drugs. However, subsequently some of the larger and more dynamic Indian enterprises such as Ranbaxy Laboratories, Dr Reddy's Labs, Cipla and Cadila, have started marketing their own formulations in different countries with the help of a growing network of overseas offices and subsidiaries set up in key international markets. USA is the biggest market for India's pharmaceutical exports accounting for 10-12 per cent of exports. The export basket of India includes generic drugs like Ibuprufen, Sulphamethoxazole, Metronidazole, Amoxycilline, Ampicilline, Mebendazole, Beta Ionone, Erythromycin, Pappain, Potassium Iodide, Brucine Salts,

Cephalexin, Ethambutol Hydrochloride, Trimethoprim etc.A study comparing the performance of MNE affiliates and domestic enterprises in Indian pharmaceutical industry over the 1990s based on a balanced sample of 76 firms (60 domestic and 16 MNE subsidiaries) found the domestic enterprises are more dynamic in terms of growth of investment and output, export-orientation, R&D activity, technology purchases from abroad and in terms of labour productivity (defined as the net value-added per rupee spent on labor). However, MNE affiliates enjoyed considerably higher profit margins because of their greater focus on more value adding formulations and their well-established brand names.

The development of process innovation capability of Indian enterprises has enabled them to introduce newer medicines within a short time lag. Most of the drugs could be introduced within 4-5 years of their introduction in the world market. The prices of these drugs in India have been much cheaper compared to rest of the world. For instance, Ranitidine, Famotidine, Astemizole, Ondansetron sell in the US market at about 50 times the Indian prices! The cheaper prices of drugs have made them affordable to the masses of poor in the country and thus have served an important social cause of providing access of modern medicine to poorer people.

The technological capabilities of Indian companies have grown to a point when leading MNEs have started to take note of it. For instance, Eli Lilly established a joint venture with Ranbaxy in the mid-1990s for development of a cost effective process for synthesis of Cefaclor, among other products, taking advantage of the latter's process development capabilities. Similarly, Bayer contracted Ranbaxy to develop single doses formulations of its proprietary Ciprofloxacine. A number of leading MNEs have also contracted Indian public funded R&D institutions for synthesis of new molecules and process development. These include Abbot Laboratories, Parke Davis, and Smith Kline and Beecham, among others, that have commissioned Indian Institute for Chemical Technologies, Hyderabad and National Chemical Laboratories, Pune. Astra (now Astra-Zeneca) has set up a full fledged R&D centre in Bangalore to draw upon trained manpower and research infrastructure available in the country, despite the fact that Indian patent regime does not provide product patents.

Thus the Indian pharmaceutical industry has evolved from one dependent upon imports and some formulation activity in the late sixties to one which is able to introduce some of the most sophisticated products indigenously produced within a relatively short lag and at a fraction of the cost, and export a growing proportion of its produce to emerge as a net foreign exchange earner. It is a remarkable.achievement especially because it has been accomplished within two decades of the change of patent regime. The case study of India, besides those of the East Asian countries, further highlights the critical importance of fine-tuning and calibrating the IPR regime to the level of development of the country.

TRIPs Regime for Developing Countries

The international environment with respect to intellectual property has changed considerably with the conclusion of the TRIPs Agreement. The TRIPs Agreement accommodates the demands of the industrialized countries for higher international standards of protection by mandating the extension of patentability to virtually all fields of technology recognized in developed country patent systems, by prolonging the patent protection for a uniform term of twenty years, and by providing legal recognition of the patentee's exclusive rights to import the patented products. The patent rights are enjoyable without discrimination as to the place of invention, the field of technology and whether products are imported or locally produced.

All the signatories to the trade negotiations are, therefore, obliged to harmonize their IPR regime and to provide product patents for pharmaceuticals and chemicals. The coverage of the patent protection has also been expanded by the provision for patents on micro-organisms and protection of plant varieties either by patents or by an effective sui generis system or by any combination thereof. The full implementation of the TRIPs Agreement is likely to have an important bearing on the patterns of development in developing countries. In what follows we briefly review some of the important dimensions of these effects.

a) Local Technological Capability Building

The strengthening and harmonization of IPR regimes worldwide has considerable implications for the process of acquisition of local technological capability by developing countries. The provision of product patents on chemical and pharmaceutical products, for instance, would adversely affect the process of innovative activity of the developing country enterprises in the manufacture of chemicals covered by patents. The development of new chemical compounds is generally beyond the capability of most developing country enterprises in view of the huge resources involved. Therefore, they focus attention on process innovations for the known chemicals and bulk drugs. This imitative duplication or reverse engineering activity is an important source of learning in developing countries. Indeed, most industrialized countries of today and newly industrialized countries encouraged local learning through soft patent laws and the absence of product patents in chemicals in the early stages of their development as highlighted earlier. It means that the poorer countries of today will not be able to benefit from an important source of total factor productivity growth (viz. absorption of spillovers of foreign inventions) that was available to countries that have developed already. In that respect the TRIPs Agreement is highly inequitable.

The probability of stronger IPR regime encouraging innovative activity in developing countries is very small. In fact the adoption of utility models or petty patents and design patents has a greater potential in encouraging local technological activity rather than implementation of the provisions of TRIPs in poorer countries.

b) Industrialization, Technology Transfers and Trade

Recent trends suggest a reversal of trend of the growing importance of arm's length licensing as a mode of technology transfer as MNEs prefer to internalize the technology transactions. The strengthening of IPRs regime may further limit the access of technology by developing country enterprises. Kim provides a number of examples of Korean corporations being denied technology licenses by patent holders in the Western world forcing them to reverse engineer the products. A number of local enterprises in developing countries will come under pressure to close down or form alliances with larger firms, resulting in a concentration of the industry. Dependence on imports may go up. Mascus and Penubarti for instance, find that TRIPs could affect import volumes significantly; e.g. in Mexico, the anticipated rise in manufactured imports could be of the magnitude of $ 6.3 billion, amounting to 9.4 per cent of its real manufactured imports in 1995.

c) Prices of medicines and loss of consumer welfare

A number of studies have examined the effect on prices of medicines after introduction of product patents and have simulated welfare losses for consumers in developing countries. It is widely believed that drug prices will go up upon introduction of product patents as happened in China which introduced them in 1993. Nogues finds the welfare losses to 6 developing countries (Argentina, Brazil, India, Mexico, Korea and Taiwan) from introduction of product patents to be between US$ 3.5 billion to $10.8 billion depending upon the assumptions. The gains to the patent owners from such introduction would range between $ 2.9 billion to $ 14.4 billion. The welfare loss to India could be between $ 1.4 billion to $ 4.2 billion in a year. Watal simulates the likely increase in pharmaceutical prices and decrease in welfare in India with the introduction of product patents in 22 existing pharmaceutical products and finds that weighted mean drug price in India could increase between 26 per cent (for a linear demand function) to 242 per cent (with a constant elasticity-type demand function). An earlier study by Subramanian had found the maximum price increase of 67 per cent for India following the introduction of product patents. Fink finds the range of price increase between 182 to 225 per cent.

That suggests that introduction of product patents would affect prices of medicines significantly and unless new drugs are more efficient, there will be a decline in the health levels of population. The recent case of huge differences between prices of HIV Aids drugs sold by patent holders in South Africa and their generic substitutes just provides an further evidence to the potential of price increases following the introduction of product patents. It may be argued that the vast majority of drugs are out of patent protection and hence will not be affected. Yet the AIDS drugs controversy shows that effective treatment for many of scourges of the day such as cancer, cardiac failures, renal problems, among others, may be affected.

d) Income transfers from developing countries

Given the near complete domination of developed countries on technology generation as evident from the 95 per cent ownership of US patents, the strengthening and harmonization of IPRs regime will lead to a substantial increase in flow of royalties and license fees from developing countries to developed countries. McCalman quantifies the impact of patent harmonization finds that it has the capacity to generate large transfers of income between countries, with US being the major beneficiary. World Bank updates the computations of McCalman and suggests that the net patent rents derived by the US (in 2000 US$) could add up to over $ 19 billion, to Germany $ 6.7 billion, and Japan $ 5.7 billion. Among the developing countries, China could see an outflow of patent rents of the order of $5.1 biliion, India $ 903 million, Israel $ 3.8 billion.

Furthermore, the extension of IPRs to plant varieties could further increase the outgo of royalties for the breeder lines of the seed companies even though the basic raw material for the development of these varieties, viz. genetic diversity which is largely found in developing countries and is supposedly the work of generations of farmers in these countries, is generally available to them free.

e) *Impact on global technological activity and availability of drugs*

One of the arguments in favour of a stronger IPR regime is based on the premise that expenditures on R&D were significantly determined by appropriability conditions. Hence, ensuring adequate appropriability with more stringent IPR protection was deemed to be a necessary condition for sustaining the pace of innovation in the global economy. The empirical literature, however, does not support this presumption as patent protection was found to be instrumental for only a small proportion of innovations.

On the other hand, studies show that spillover effects of R&D activity of other firms to be a lot more important in inducing firms to undertake R&D compared to appropriability. The R&D outputs of other firms form valuable inputs for the R&D efforts of these firms. Hence, tightening of IPRs is likely to affect innovative activity adversely by stifling these spillovers. Therefore, it is by no means clear that strengthening of IPRs will increase innovative activity even in the developed world especially for solving the problems and diseases faced by developing countries. As World Bank cautions 'there is now a risk of excessively strict IPRs adversely affecting follow-on innovations and actually slowing down the pace of (technological development)'. Furthermore, the research priorities of MNEs are determined by the purchasing power and very little R&D is currently done on tropical diseases. Unless some steps are taken by the international community, such as those discussed by the recent report of WHO's Commission on Macroeconomics and Health

(CMH), the pattern is not likely to change significantly in the future.

Issues for National and International Action

The preceding discussion suggests that the ongoing trend of strengthening and harmonization of IPR regime is going to affect the process of development of poorer countries in a significant manner by choking an important contributor of growth that has been variously described as imitative duplication, reverse engineering or knowledge spillovers from abroad. It is also likely to affect the prices of a large number of important drugs and thus affect the health systems in poorer countries. It would lead to income transfers from poorer to richer countries. It is likely to adversely affect the manufacturing activity in developing countries and may increase their imports but does not guarantee increased in FDI inflows, access to technology or R&D investments in tropical diseases. These challenges require a response at the national policy levels as well as a response from the international community. In what follows, we outline some of the policy responses that could help in moderating the adverse effects of TRIPs Agreement on developing countries.

Policy responses to be taken at the national level

a) Incorporating the Provisions of Compulsory Licensing in the IPR Legislation: Developing countries should build adequate provisions for compulsory licensing in their IPR legislation in order to safeguard them from possible abuses of monopoly power obtained by patent owners. The compulsory licenses are permitted under Article 31 of the TRIPs Agreement.

The Agreement does not limit the grounds upon whch compulsory licenses may be granted and only sets forth the conditions to be applied in the case of granting. This includes specification of grounds of compulsory licensing and the reasonable rates of licensing fees. Recent withdrawal of proceedings by the US against Brazil's compulsory licensing provisions show that intelligently crafted domestic patent laws can meet national objectives and yet be TRIPs compatible.

b) *Incorporating the Research Exception:* Developing countries could incorporate provisions allowing researchers to use a patented invention for research, in order to understand the invention more fully. Experimentation on a patented invention is clearly admissible as an exception to exclusive rights under Article 30.

c) *Early Working Exception or 'Bolar' Provision:* It is possible to make provision for allowing manufacturers of generic drugs to use the patented invention to obtain marketing approval without patent owner's permission and before the expiration of patent. This facilitates the generic manufacturers to market their products as soon as the patent expires. This provision is sometimes called the regulatory exception or Bolar provision under Article 8. The US, Canada, Australia, Israel and Argentina have adopted Bolar exception in their patent legislation.

d) *Resisting the Attempts to Evolve TRIPs Plus Regime and Ever-greening of Patents:* Developed countries are constantly putting pressure on developing countries to implement stricter patent legislation than required under TRIPs, exclude compulsory licensing, parallel imports provisions and include provisions that would result in increasing the life of the patent (ever-greening), as well as grant data exclusivity to them. The TRIPs Agreement however, is clear that a new use for an old formulation does not constitute an inventive step (Art. 27(1)). Therefore, member countries are within their rights not to permit the practice of ever-greening of patents.

e) *Allowing Parallel Imports or Grey-Market Imports:* Since 'exhaustion of rights' issue cannot be raised in the dispute settlement under TRIPs Agreement, developing countries should allow parallel imports or grey-market imports. The experience of several countries suggests that substantial costs savings could result from such imports because of differential pricing strategy practiced by MNEs depending upon the extent of competition in different markets.

f) *Competition Policy:* The patent system grants temporary monopolies to the firms that introduce innovations. The national competition or antitrust policies are needed to prevent the build up of excessive monopoly power of certain enterprises and to deal with possible abuse of monopoly power emanating from patent protection. The TRIPs Agreement (Articles 8 and 40, Section 8) explicitly provides for appropriate measures to prevent the abuse of IPRs or the resort to anti-competitive practices. Apparently in the US, 'compulsory licensing has been specified as a remedy in more than 100 anti-trust cases making available some 40,000 to 50,000 patents at reasonable or no royalties'.

g) *Incorporating Breeders Exceptions and Farmers Exceptions in sui generis Plant Variety Protection:* TRIPs Agreement allows flexibility to the member countries to exclude plant varieties from the scope of patent protection and instead opt for an effective sui generis system. In order to minimize the adverse effect on the plant breeding programmes and protecting small and marginal farmers from buying seeds who typically save them for the next crop, developing countries could build provisions for exceptions for farmers and plant breeders.

h) *Price Controls for Essential Drugs:* To protect the poor masses from the price increases following the introduction of product patents, governments may impose regulation of prices of essential drugs. To keep the price controls effective, transparent formula for evolving them could be made providing for a reasonable mark-up over the cost. Indian experience shows that price controls have proved to be effective means of keeping prices of life saving essential drugs under check. However, given the possibility of transfer pricing manipulation, there may be complications in administering price controls for imported drugs.

i) *Introduce Utility Models and Industrial Design Patents:* The experience of several East Asian countries suggests that petty patents and industrial design patents could be effective means of encouraging domestic enterprises to undertake minor adaptive innovations and foster a innovation based rivalry among them.

Policy responses at the international level

The recent controversy concerning the HIV AIDS drugs in South Africa, among other factors, has helped to focus attention of the international community on the possible adverse effects of the implementation of TRIPs Agreement on poorer countries. Over the past year a number of international initiatives have been taken to deal with the matter. These include establishment of the Commission on Macroeconomics and Health by the WHO and Commission on IPRs by the British Government. WHO and WTO organized a Workshop on Differential Pricing and Financing of Essential Drugs at Hosbjor, April 2001. The Fourth Ministerial Meeting in Doha in November 2001 adopted a Declaration on TRIPs Agreement and Public Health. UNDP's Human Development Report 2001 as well as World Bank's Global Economic Prospects 2002 reports focused on the IPRs and their impact for developing countries. However, these initiatives are yet to lead to a concrete outcome addressing the many problems that are raised by the TRIPs Agreement. In what follows we summarize a few avenues for possible international action.

a) *Moratorium on further strengthening of IPR regime:* There is tendency in some developed countries to treat provisions of TRIPs as the minimum standards and are constantly attempting to evolve stronger norms through unilateral or bilateral approaches. A consensus needs to be built on the need to put a moratorium on such approaches for the next couple of decades or so.

b) *Granting flexibility to developing countries in implementing the provisions of TRIPs:* Most of the adverse effects concerning TRIPs on poor countries arise not because of IPR regimes but from the attempt to harmonize them across the countries at different levels of development. Thhere is also a discussion whether TRIPs should fundamentally belong to

WTO. However, the least that could be done is allowing flexibility to developing countries to implement the provisions of the Agreement as and when their level of development has reached a certain stage. This could be achieved if a consensus among the developed countries is built on the differential need of developing countries for IPR regime 6 . A possible revision of TRIPs could incorporate a provision that grants to developing countries a flexibility to implement the TRIPs obligations until they reach a per capita income of the level of US$ 1000, for instance. Another possibility could be to shorten the term of product patents applicable to low income countries. This way the Agreement would have incorporated development dimension. The Commission's work could be instrumental in building such a consensus.

c) *Incorporating Specific Provisions for Transfer of Technology:* The TRIPs Agreement pays an inadequate attention to the transfer of technology. Access to technology is increasingly become difficult for developing countries, as observed earlier. There is need for defining conditions, norms and practices for facilitating transfers of technology for production of essential drugs and other critical inputs.

d) *International Funding R&D Activity in Low Income Countries:* One of the ways of compensating the low income countries for the adverse effects of strengthened IPR regime is to provide increased technical assistance and R&D funding to local enterprises to help them build local capabilities. One possibility in this-respect could be that developed countries donate (a substantial proportion of) technology license fees collected from low income countries to a fund created in the respective countries to assist inventive activities of domestic enterprises. Furthermore, there is need to address the issue of funding R&D on special problems and tropical diseases that concern low income countries. It has been widely acknowledged that global pharmaceutical industry has neglected research on tropical diseases. The CMH has recommended a donor commitment of $ 27 billion per annum for the health needs of low-income countries including $ 3 billion per annum for R&D for diseases of the poor. It is arguable that this funding of $ 3 billion could also help to moderate some adverse effects on the inventive activity in low-income countries if it is awarded to institutions and enterprises based in these countries. Therefore, an additional recommendation could be made in conjunction with those of CMH that the funds would allocated to eligible and competent institutions and companies of low income countries.

e) *Differential Pricing:* There has been a lot of discussion on the possibility of improving the access of poorer countries to patented medicines through differential pricing. There are a number of practical issues concerned with the differential pricing that need to be resolved.

Bibliography

Azarchs, Tanya (2000). *The Internet's Impact on Financial Services,* Standard & Poor's CreditWeek, Jan. 26.

Bank Network News (2000). *Virtual Banks Get Physical With ATMs* 18, 21, March 30.

Barth, James R., Daniel E. Nolle, and Tara N. Rice (2000). *Commercial Banking Structure, Regulation, and Performance: An International Comparison, in Modernizing Financial Systems,* edited by Dimitri B. Papadimitriou, St. Martin's Press, Inc.

Carlson, Tina (2000). *One CU's Secret: Lack of Technology,* The Credit Union Journal, March 6.

Costanzo, Chris, and Adriana Senior (1999). *Banks Opting for Discrete Web Units,* American Banker, December 6.

Couch, Karen, and Donna L. Parker (2000). *Net Interest' Grows as Banks Rush Online.*

Daudelin, Art (2000). *Wingspan Losing Altitude*? Bank Technology News 13, 1, January.

Day, Kathleen (2000). *Web-Only Banks Start to Get Real,* Washington Post, March 31.

Egland, Kori L., Karen Furst, Daniel E. Nolle, and Douglas Robertson (1998). *Banking Over the Internet,* Quarterly Journal 17, 4, Office of the Comptroller of the Currency, December.

Furst, Karen, William W. Lang, and Daniel E. Nolle (1998). *Technological Innovation in Banking and Payments: Industry Trends and Implications for Banks,* Quarterly Journal 17, 3, Office of the Comptroller of the Currency, December.

Hallerman, David (1999a). *Spinning a New Web of Online Banking,* Bank Technology News 12, 7, July.

Hitt, Lorin M., and Frances X. Frei (1999). Do Better Customers Utilize Electronic Distribution Channels? *The Case of PC Banking,* Wharton Financial Institutions Center, Working Paper Series No. 99-21, April.

Hitt, Lorin M., Frances X. Frei, and Patrick T. Harker (1999). *How Financial Firms Decide on Technology,* Brookings-Wharton Papers on Financial Services: 1999.

Horsfield, Richard (2000). *Shaping the future of online financial services,* The Banker, January.

Marks, James (1999). *The Impact of the Internet on Users and Suppliers of Financial Services,* Brookings-Wharton Papers on Financial Services: 1999.

Moody's Investors Service (2000a). *The Internet and U.S. Banks,"* January.

O'Sullivan, Orla (1998). *Technology Spending's Uncertain Payoff,* U.S. Banker, September.

Pizzani, Lori (1999). *Web Offerings Lure Small Businesses,* Bank Technology News 12, 3, March.

Radecki, Lawrence J., John Wenninger, and Daniel K. Orlow (1997) *'Industry Structure: Electronic Delivery's Potential Effects on Retail Banking,* Journal of Retail Banking Services, 19, 4, Winter.

Robertson, Douglas, Jim Cambruzzi, Kevin Jacques, Peter Nigro, Bill Pate, Hugh Rich, and Art Steele (2000). *Large Bank Retirement Services: A Comparative Practices Study.*

Timewell, Stephen and Kung Young (2000). "*Online surge blasts banks,*" The Banker, January.

Toonkel, Jessica (2000a). *Compubank, Failing to Excite Public, Eyes On-Line Service for Businesses,* American Banker, March 3.

United States General Accounting Office (1998). *Electronic Banking: Experiences Reported by Banks in Implementing On-line Banking,* GAO/GGD-98-34, January.

Index